TURNAROUND LEADERSHIP

TURNAROUND LEADERSHIP
MAKING DECISIONS, REBUILDING TRUST AND DELIVERING RESULTS AFTER A CRISIS

SHAUN O'CALLAGHAN

KoganPage
LONDON PHILADELPHIA NEW DELHI

For the real Quartet:
Ellie, Matthew, Michael and Alice

Publisher's note

Every possible effort has been made to ensure that the information contained in this book is accurate at the time of going to press, and the publishers and author cannot accept responsibility for any errors or omissions, however caused. No responsibility for loss or damage occasioned to any person acting, or refraining from action, as a result of the material in this publication can be accepted by the editor, the publisher or the author.

First published in Great Britain and the United States in 2010 by Kogan Page Limited

Apart from any fair dealing for the purposes of research or private study, or criticism or review, as permitted under the Copyright, Designs and Patents Act 1988, this publication may only be reproduced, stored or transmitted, in any form or by any means, with the prior permission in writing of the publishers, or in the case of reprographic reproduction in accordance with the terms and licences issued by the CLA. Enquiries concerning reproduction outside these terms should be sent to the publishers at the undermentioned addresses:

120 Pentonville Road	525 South 4th Street, #241	4737/23 Ansari Road
London N1 9JN	Philadelphia PA 19147	Daryaganj
United Kingdom	USA	New Delhi 110002
www.koganpage.com		India

© Shaun O'Callaghan, 2010

The right of Shaun O'Callaghan to be identified as the author of this work has been asserted by him in accordance with the Copyright, Designs and Patents Act 1988.

ISBN   978 0 7494 5709 9
E-ISBN 978 0 7494 5748 8

British Library Cataloguing-in-Publication Data

A CIP record for this book is available from the British Library.

Library of Congress Cataloging-in-Publication Data

O'Callaghan, Shaun.
  Turnaround leadership : making decisions, rebuilding trust, and delivering results after a crisis / Shaun O'Callaghan.
    p. cm.
  Includes bibliographical references.
  ISBN 978-0-7494-5709-9 — ISBN 978-0-7494-5748-8 (ebook) 1. Crisis management. 2. Organizational change. 3. Leadership. I. Title.
  HD49.O25 2010
  658.4'092–dc22
                                                              2010000353

Typeset by Graphicraft Limited, Hong Kong
Printed and bound in India by Replika Press Pvt Ltd

Contents

Acknowledgements	*viii*
1. Leading after a crisis	**1**
Introduction	1
Making the right promises	6
Gathering multiple new viewpoints	8
Core business skills	10
Delivering results through relationships	13
Rebuilding trust with authentic communication	16
Next steps	18
2. What is a crisis?	**21**
What do we mean by crisis?	21
Triggers of a crisis	22
Preventing a crisis	31
3. External causes of a crisis	**33**
Economic cycles	35
Customer priorities	39
Product, technology and business model innovation	43
Outside intervention	48

4. Internal drivers of a crisis	**53**
Broken promises	54
Corporate breakdown	59
Management optimism	69
Lack of sensitivity	71
5. Where to start after a crisis – making the right promises	**75**
Where to start – earning the right	76
Making the right promises	81
6. Gathering multiple new viewpoints	**89**
Customer aces	94
Making promises you can keep	99
Follow the money	106
Lean not mean	112
Flesh and blood	115
Imagine new futures	119
7. Core business skills 1 – cash and time	**125**
Managing cash flow and time	126
8. Core business skills 2	**149**
Developing strategy after a crisis	151
Maintaining sales	154
Cost base restructuring	157
9. Delivering results through relationships	**161**
Overview	165
Results	169
Actions	171
Operating model	174
Possibilities and relationships	176

10.	**Rebuilding trust with authentic communication**	**179**
	Trust	181
	Benefits less costs = value	184
	Intimacy	187
	Perceived risk	189
	Trust and communication	191
	Last words	191
	References	*193*
	Index	*195*

Acknowledgements

I would like to thank all the people I have met and worked with around the world of business, turnaround and restructuring. From cleaning the toilets at a factory in Japan with the chief executive before the workers arrived for their shift to answering calls with new graduates at a call centre in Bangalore.

The book would never have happened without the support of Emma and the QRL girls. In particular, for doing most of the hard work and for always being there, the biggest thanks have to go to Karen.

The views in this book are those of the author and do not represent the views of any organization.

1 Leading after a crisis

Introduction

Any company that is being built to exist for more than a generation will have to go through periods of significant market uncertainty and suffer recession or business crisis. Any manager that wants to take up a leadership position will face a business crisis at some point in their career. In fact some leaders make it their career to help companies recover after a crisis. The simple fact is that if you are in business for any reasonable period of time you will have to manage and lead through a crisis. Crises can come in many shapes and sizes: system-wide and sector-specific problems can arise from a recession, technology changes rendering a business model obsolete, regulatory changes and shifts in customer spending habits. Company-specific problems may result from poor strategic choices, lack of financial discipline, failed implementation of an IT project, or self-inflicted damage to a brand.

Whilst an insightful understanding of the causes of a crisis is an essential ingredient for building a viable recovery plan, something extra will be required from you. That 'something extra' can make the difference between not recovering from a crisis and using the crisis to become a stronger business. It is the 'something extra' that we will be looking at in this book.

The objectives of the book are twofold. First, to enable leaders to identify the drivers of a potential crisis and so take actions to avoid one. Second, to help executives rebuild their business after a crisis. The skills, training and experiences you will have already accumulated during your career will be highly relevant to planning and delivering a successful recovery. The question is whether there is something extra you can do to improve the chances of success. In this book we shall look at the issue of leadership after a crisis and what can be done to develop the particular skills required during a recovery phase. We concentrate on five areas of 'leadership expertise' that a manager can seek to master to be more effective in recovering after a crisis:

1. making the right promises;
2. gathering multiple new viewpoints;
3. core business skills;
4. delivering results through relationships;
5. rebuilding trust with authentic communication.

Let us briefly consider each of these areas of expertise. As a leader after a crisis you must next decide what, if any, promises to make and to which stakeholders. In periods of crisis and their aftermath there will always be higher levels of uncertainty about the future. Perversely, in such periods of heightened uncertainty people crave more certainty. Everybody asks for more and more detail and budgets and forecasts are redone at more frequent intervals. In such circumstances understanding the perspectives of your customers, investors, lenders, employees and suppliers is a key part of devising, communicating and delivering a successful recovery plan. Such understanding will help you to make promises that are balanced between the often conflicting demands of different stakeholders and that can be kept.

The second area of leadership expertise we will consider is gathering multiple new viewpoints. It is often the lack of a fully rounded view of the issues that results in a business crisis. As you plan to emerge from the immediate impact of a crisis it is essential that a diverse, but appropriate, range of viewpoints is gathered to inform your recovery plan, communication and implementation. A critical aspect is not just gathering the differing viewpoints but being able to understand how the viewpoints interact with each other. We shall refer to this as 'the view from the top of the mountain'. During the period of crisis many people will be using very directive forms of leadership, which are often important to ensure urgent stabilization actions are taken quickly. However, recovery from a crisis requires reflection on the causes of the problems and the opportunities for change. Rather than taking a 'Just Do It' approach, it may be helpful to stop and think for a while.

The third area of leadership expertise is developing the core business skills which will help you make the right judgements and plans for a recovery. These may be skills that you have already developed and use in 'normal' business circumstances but their application to a post-crisis environment may require you to refresh your insights. Areas that are covered in this book include developing strategy after a crisis, maintaining sales, cost base restructuring and cash flow management.

The fourth area of leadership expertise covers how you can affect the delivery of business results. At a certain tier of management you become unable to directly deliver results through the impact of your own efforts. At this point working longer and longer hours, with ever more intensity and enthusiasm, will not produce the returns that it did earlier in your career. By this stage you will need to have made the transition from delivering results by yourself to enabling other people to be more capable and motivated in their jobs. This realization and skill is heavily tested in the period after a crisis. You will be relying on people within and outside your organization to deliver results in a period of high uncertainty, often with unclear short-term rewards. This requires your leadership skill, or more correctly your ability to persuade others to follow you, to be practised and credible.

Each of the four areas of leadership expertise described above requires your thoughtful and skilled communication to rebuild trust with people inside and outside your organization. To be effective such communication needs to be authentic. During a crisis people will often have seen into the 'laundry basket' of your business and its operations. Pretending that things are different or ignoring the issues that people actually want to discuss is unlikely to restore much confidence. The insights in this area are firstly remembering that stakeholders are actually people made of flesh and blood and secondly categorizing the rebuilding of trust into practical but focused actions.

Together these five areas of leadership expertise are the levers that a manager can use to make a positive difference to a business and its people after a crisis. We will look at each of these five areas and identify practical responses for leaders to drive a turnaround. This chapter aims to provide only an overview of our approach. Chapter 2 considers what a crisis is and how to prevent one from occurring. Chapters 3 and 4 examine the external causes and internal drivers of a crisis. In Chapter 5 we will discuss how to start to build a recovery plan and the first leadership expertise area of making the right promises. Chapters 6 to 10 look at each of the other four areas of leadership expertise described above, including tools, ideas and case studies relevant to each that you can use to engage your people.

The essential question to ask at this stage is how confident are you and your team in each of these areas of leadership expertise and is that confidence well placed? Some questions to ask yourself and your team around these areas are:

Making the right promises In our current situation do we understand what all our key stakeholders are focusing on and the promises they are seeking from us and our company?

Gathering multiple new viewpoints As leaders, have we taken a complete 360 degree view of the business, its stakeholders and the market in the current environment? A failure to consider all perspectives may restrict the range of ideas and solutions that are available.

Core business skills Do we have the necessary expertise, experience and insights to make decisions about the issues that matter most in our post-crisis situation?

Delivering results through relationships What are the right implementation models and leadership styles to employ to ensure that the promises we make are delivered?

Rebuilding trust through authentic communication How will we build and maintain the level of trust with employees, customers, suppliers, lenders and investors that will be necessary to deliver the recovery plan?

As the book explores each of these areas of leadership expertise, you should consider whether you and your team have sufficient competence to be successful leaders in each particular area. In addition, you should consider whether the business as a whole has the necessary competence and whether sufficient priority is being given to each area. By using the five expertise areas to provide guidance and coaching to your teams, you can start to provide increased levels of certainty about the future despite the uncertainties in your business following a crisis. Let us consider in a little more detail the issues of and approach to each of the five leadership expertise areas. Each area includes tools for making practical choices and decisions for your business recovery.

Making the right promises

In the normal course of business, a leader is constantly making and trying to deliver on a set of promises to key stakeholders. In many ways you could say that the principal role of a leader is to make, balance and deliver on promises such as these: What can and should I promise to investors and lenders to attract and retain the right financing? What will customers expect and require from our company in order for them to continue to buy from us? How can I attract, motivate and retain the right people? What will suppliers want from me and what can I promise them?

The tool we use in this leadership expertise area considers four types of stakeholder. First, the customer and consumer. Promises to customers include the quality of the product or service offering and its price, availability and functionality. A company will often make both explicit – for instance, the price – and implicit promises to a customer. These implicit promises can become very important during and after a corporate crisis. For example, customers may consider whether buying one of your products at a time when creditors have concerns about your viability makes them look foolish in front of their colleagues or friends. The second stakeholder group we consider is investors and lenders. This group provides finance in the shape of equity, bonds, bank facilities and letters of credit that allow the business to operate. Hard promises to this group tend to be financial in nature, for example, dividend expectations, loan interest payments, covenant compliance and expected share value creation. However, investors and lenders are also increasingly interested in the brand and supply chain integrity of the companies they invest in. The third group is the staff of the company. The promises to employees can include a salary or wage, a safe and equitable place to work, development opportunities and consultation. After a crisis, your people will be the ones you need to design and deliver a recovery and you may have to make and keep promises to them that were not necessary in less turbulent times. The fourth, and last, stakeholder group we will consider is suppliers. This group includes trade suppliers and their credit insurers and organizations that supply your company with a 'licence' to operate, such as regulators and governments. The manager and leader's job is to balance all these promises, as illustrated in Figure 1.1.

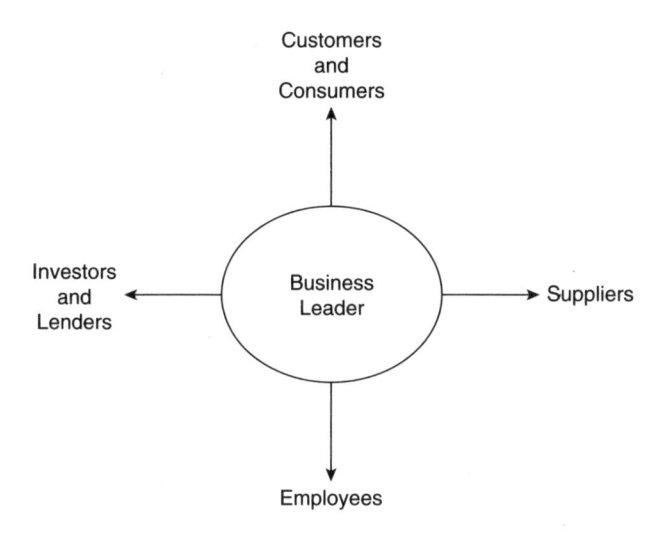

Figure 1.1 Leadership wobble board

The business leader sits in the middle of each group's expectations and tries to balance the promises made and delivered to each of them. At any time the situation is probably unbalanced in favour of one or more of the stakeholder groups. However, the promises need to balance out over the medium-term, otherwise the business is likely to create and then face a crisis. For example, many customers might like to receive a top quality product for no charge, forever. It is unlikely that a company providing such a proposition would be able to pay dividends, interest, salaries or suppliers. A leader is always adjusting the balance and seeking new ways and ideas that can increase the overall value to all of the stakeholders and maintain a medium-term balanced position. An analogy which describes this skill is learning to use a 'balance board' or 'wobble board' at the gym. These round boards, with a half sphere on their underside, require the user to balance and constantly alter his or her weight distribution in order to keep the board flat and upright. Initially, this can feel very uncomfortable and be difficult to achieve. As with almost all new skills it requires practice, discipline and often some coaching. Balancing the often competing interests of customers, investors and lenders, employees and suppliers requires a leader to develop new skills and expertise. Mastering this balance in times of stable markets and favourable economic conditions is quite a test. In times of crisis there are additional challenges analogous to people kicking the wobble board at unexpected times. To deliver a recovery after a crisis will require you to be more than 'good enough' at balancing the expectations and promises made to stakeholders; you will need to master this leadership skill.

Gathering multiple new viewpoints

The proposition here is that in order to make the best leadership decisions after a crisis you need to consider the factors facing your business from multiple viewpoints. In addition, you need to be able to understand how those multiple views interact with each other. For example, if you come from a marketing background then it is most natural to see the business issues and potential solutions to a crisis through the filter of a marketing professional. Accountants might see the problems and challenges through a financial viewpoint in much the same way as store detectives are reputed to see only potential shoplifters rather than customers. I rang a colleague recently to ask about a new client he was working with. I asked how big the company was, expecting him to tell me its turnover. He told me how many employees it has. I trained as an accountant; he is an HR professional.

If you can hold multiple viewpoints of your business and market and help your teams to do the same, you open up the possibility of generating more innovative and deliverable actions. If you accept the need to take a 360 degree view of your business the question then arises: what are the different viewpoints you need to consider?

The tool we will use in this leadership expertise area is inspired by the popular family game of Trivial Pursuit™. Six viewpoints are examined and you and your team need to test yourselves and assess whether you have sufficient knowledge to answer the questions that arise (see Figure 1.2).

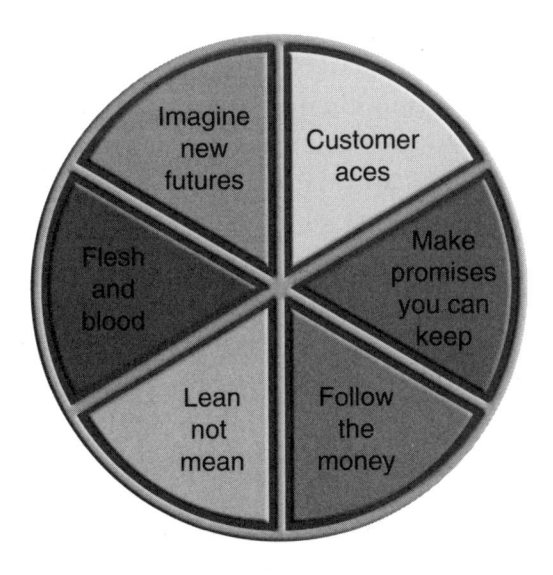

Figure 1.2 Six view points model

The six viewpoints in the tool are:

- *Customer aces.* How will consumers and enterprises behave during and after the crisis?
- *Make promises you can keep.* How are plans and decisions made and do we deliver on our promises?

- *Follow the money.* Where and how is cash generated and used within our business?
- *Lean not mean.* How is our cost base structured and what could be done to change it?
- *Flesh and blood.* How will the people outside and inside our business be affected by the crisis and how might they react?
- *Imagine new futures.* As we look towards a recovery, what are the transformational changes that our company could make following the crisis?

It is important to consider the whole of your business from each particular viewpoint. For example, when considering the customer aces viewpoint it is not sufficient just to look at products, pricing and service. Customers will also have a view on management, supply chain, cost structures, your values and finances and the future. You must consider a customer's total view of your business and the market to start to gain valuable insights for your recovery plan. There may be additional, or more relevant, viewpoints for you and your teams to understand in respect of your particular industry or geography. For example, the attitude of governments and regulators may be a critical viewpoint for you to assess. The important elements of this tool are that you, as a leader, take the time to articulate the no more than six or seven viewpoints that need to be assessed and can explain the impact of each to your team. In Chapter 6, each of the viewpoints set out above will be considered, together with methods for gaining insights into each.

Core business skills

The third area of leadership expertise is developing the core business skills which will help you make the right judgements and plans for a recovery. As a leader after a crisis you will have to draw upon a diverse range of business skills and experience in order to deliver a successful recovery. In this book we focus on a few of those skills that have particular relevance to leading after a crisis:

- cash flow and time management;
- developing strategy after a crisis;
- maintaining sales;
- cost base restructuring.

During the stabilization period following a crisis and in building the recovery plan, there are two resources that are of life-and-death importance to the business: cash and time. These two resources are also interdependent. You will need sufficient cash flow to buy yourself time to build a credible recovery plan and to sell that plan to your key stakeholders. You need sufficient time to understand how to increase cash generation internally within your business and raise new sources of finance. Any approach to cash management has to address the issue of 'time' management as well. We will look at the different phases of cash and time management during and after a crisis and at how these tools can be used to rebuild confidence with key stakeholders. It is important to consider not only the direct benefits of better cash flow management – more cash and more time – but also the indirect benefit of improving management's reputation for being in control. Even when better cash management is not a critical survival issue, it may be valuable to demonstrate a mastery of the cash position of your business as this can increase confidence in your ability to recover from the crisis. We shall discuss later the many positive leadership benefits deriving from mastering cash management that are hard to replicate from other sources and that the hard work required to master your cash flow is normally too much for most managers to contemplate. By examining what is required to become an expert in cash flow leadership, you can at least decide whether it is something that you and your organization want to undertake. We will talk a lot about these issues in Chapter 7.

After the initial stabilization phase following a crisis, when sufficient time and cash has been secured to consider the medium-term future of the business, you will have to start to develop a future strategy for the company. As much as a crisis places great strain on a business and its people, it can also provide the opportunity to fundamentally redefine what the business does and how it operates. There may be opportunities to exit certain markets, close operations, change service priorities or create a truly customer-centric culture. Such once-in-a-generation opportunities arise partly because you are under pressure to 'do something' and 'take strong action' from stakeholders. The smart thing to do is to use this licence for change to do the things that will have lasting longer-term impact. The easy thing to do is to cave in to what others are demanding, even when you know it is the wrong thing to be doing. Your strategy development needs to balance the rational and the pragmatic and we shall examine a process to help you achieve this balance in Chapter 8.

The financial dynamic of most companies' profit and loss accounts is that the revenue line is much more variable than the cost line. Even within the variable costs of goods, elements, such as raw materials, have to be bought some time in advance, tying up cash in working capital. This mismatch between the speed of a potential decline in demand and an ability to reduce costs correspondingly can turn a small problem into a full-blown liquidity crisis in just a short space of time. This makes maintaining sales during and after a crisis one of the most important things to focus on to help the business recover. Some sectors in particular can experience rapid swings in customer demand. Leisure spending in bars, restaurants and hotels can decline overnight if a crisis appears to threaten customer safety. Airlines and tour operators are subject to an immediate impact from health scares, political uncertainty and concerns about a company's financial strength. In Chapter 8 we consider how the leader of a business can enable and motivate its people and partners to continue to produce revenue.

The flip side of striving to maintain sales income is to restructure the cost base to reflect the impact of the crisis and the proposed recovery strategy. Questions that need to be considered about costs after a crisis include whether you focus on absolute total costs, variable costs, fixed costs or marginal costs. Should you be establishing programmes and projects to restructure the cost base, the first response of most companies, or enabling people to better manage costs as an ongoing way of life, less used and not well understood? It is an uncomfortable truth but if you have just been through a crisis you are much more likely to suffer another in the next 12 months. As we consider the best ways to approach the cost base, perhaps it would be worthwhile considering this and selecting an approach that builds more agility into your organization. These alternative approaches to cost base restructuring are discussed in more detail in Chapter 8.

Delivering results through relationships

Achieving what has been set out in the recovery plan is the single most important part of restoring confidence after a crisis. In uncertain times the regular, 'dull' delivery of results within expectations is what people most want to hear but after a crisis it is often very difficult to make confident assumptions about the future. Given this, your leadership expertise in extracting the best possible delivery from your organization in difficult circumstances will be critical to the success of the recovery. This is the fourth area of leadership expertise that we explore. Some hold the opinion that turnaround management is a tough, directive skill that requires harsh words and sharp elbows. It is certainly true that leaders will need to work and take difficult decisions under much higher levels of scrutiny and stress than they might have been used to. You will also need to set a direction and purpose for the recovery that employees will want to follow. In addition, there is often conflict between investors, lenders and other creditors as to how any pain in the recovery plan is shared out. I would argue that all these factors call for a leader who is extremely sensitive to relationship building and management, more so than would be necessary in stable conditions.

As with the other five areas of leadership expertise, we use one principal tool to investigate the challenge of delivering results after a crisis. The tool is summarised in Figure 1.3 below.

```
        Results
       Actions
    Operating model
     Possibilities
     Relationships
```

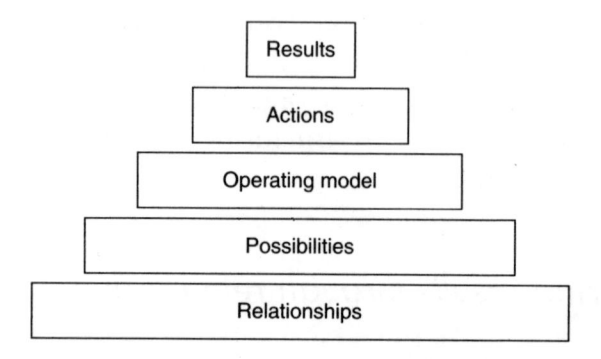

Figure 1.3 Relationships to results pyramid

I first came across a version of this tool while working as a director of a retail company being advised by a former NASA medical doctor, Jerry Joiner. The tool is intended to help senior management teams consider the activities they need to focus on to deliver business results. It provides a framework for considering how strategy is translated into results, without using the 'strategy' word.

The theory behind this approach is based on the proposition that business results can only be achieved by taking actions and the actions that are taken determine the results that are achieved. This must be true: no matter how long I sit and look at a sales forecast for the year I will not actually sell anything. One of a leader's key roles after a crisis is to set clear goals and milestones that have relevance to the actual situation of the business. If your key performance indicators do not change in any way from the time before the crisis to the period after the crisis you may need to ask if the right things are being measured. If the results are below expectation, it is the leader's job to instigate a revised set of actions and/or re-set expectations. Thoughtful and successful actions result from having the right operating model in place. The operating model includes the organizational structure of the business, the skill and motivation of the people in relevant roles, performance management and incentivization, processes and IT systems, leadership and people development.

The overall design and updating of the operating model to reflect the crisis, market developments and changing opportunities is the top team's responsibility. The right design for the operating model should be inspired by the quality and range of possibilities that are open to the business. These include which customers and markets to serve, the range and type of products and services to offer and developments in, for example, IT that affect how products and services are delivered. The operating model needs to reflect the post-crisis environment, which may require a short-term fix followed by transition to a new operating model. Once again, the role of the leadership team is to ensure that the right number and quality of new possibilities are being generated and that legacy structures that are no longer viable do not preclude development of the right operating model. The final part of the approach looks at the sources for ideas and new possibilities. The proposition is that it is the relationships that exist within a business and between a business, its customers, suppliers and other stakeholders that drive innovation and new opportunities. The role of the leader is to ensure that within the business the right quality and scope of relationships are being established.

I have mentioned above that once managers reach a certain level of seniority within a business they are unable to directly influence results by their own hard work. A former CEO of a large US retail chain explained how most of his company's customer experience was delivered by transient students working part-time to pay their way through college. Neither he nor his senior managers could serve every customer personally. They had to achieve the results they wanted through their relationships with other people, regional managers, store managers, team leaders and front-line employees. The CEO and senior managers could only deliver results by improving their relationships with their front line staff, by making their people more capable in their jobs. In a crisis you will often have to make great demands of both your employees and external stakeholders. To make others want to follow and support your recovery plan will require considerable leadership expertise in developing relationships.

Rebuilding trust with authentic communication

This is the last of the five areas of leadership expertise in our model to help with planning and delivering a successful recovery plan after a crisis. The type and quality of relationships you will require to support you in leading a successful recovery must derive from a sufficient level of trust with various stakeholders. After a crisis, however, trust levels between the company, its customers, employees, suppliers and financial stakeholders can be at dangerously low levels. This lack of trust can lead to cash and time problems, missing out on opportunities when an upturn happens and, very often, a change of management. When trust is at a low level and you need to rebuild it in order to deliver a recovery plan, the only lever to pull is improved communication. After a crisis this communication must not be anything other than authentic, as people will be watching you carefully to see if your words match the reality of the situation and your actions match your words. The issue of trust in business is much discussed and is almost universally agreed to be an essential part of a recovery plan but explaining to a team member what trust actually is and, more importantly, what actions can be taken to improve it is a challenge for many managers. The tool that we will use to develop leadership expertise in this area is based on a very practical approach to rebuilding trust. The original trust equation work was developed by David Maister *et al* (2000), looking at relationships in the professional services sector. In this book I shall use this version, adapted by business consultant and advisor, Yuda Tuval (see Figure 1.4).

$$\text{Trust} = \frac{(\text{Benefit} - \text{Cost}) \times \text{Intimacy}}{\text{Perceived Risk}}$$

Figure 1.4 Trust equation

The equation seeks to categorize actions that can be taken to improve the level of trust in a relationship. It illustrates how trust may be reduced when the other party cannot see any benefit to them from the relationship or the financial and non-financial costs of support are too high. Alternatively, whilst the rational value of the relationship may be clear enough – the benefit minus the cost – not enough time has been spent with the other person, in the right way, to build a personal bond of business intimacy. Even if you have developed the most sensible recovery plan in the history of business, you cannot just send it out by e-mail and expect everybody to align behind it and give their full support. Perhaps you have a good plan and you have spent the necessary engagement time with the relevant stakeholders, in the right way to build up a high level of trust, but this will all be diminished by the risks the other party perceives in your plans. These are not necessarily the risks that actually exist, nor those you think might exist. These are the risks that the other person thinks they see. Such perceived risks can be rational, such as concerns over debt levels, but they may also be reputational and very deeply held. For example, a particular supplier may be thinking: 'By supporting this recovery plan will I face criticism from my boss, who has never really trusted the management team involved in this company?'

The equation aims to focus your communication efforts in the right places: on the business case – benefits minus costs; the type of communication – intimacy, and the concerns – perceived risk. The next question is how to construct authentic communication that people will believe in and will pass on to others. There are a number of techniques and ideas for this which we discuss further in Chapter 10. Things to bear in mind for now are that people tend to remember stories better than bullet points, conversations happen via a series of questions and answers rather than a lecture with PowerPoint slides and the most important part of the communication will occur when you are not there. After the bank meeting to present your recovery plan, when you have long since returned to your own office, your bank manager has a cup of coffee with the head of risk at the bank. The head of risk asks your banker what his feeling is about the recovery plan that you presented. Your bank manager has a maximum of two minutes in which to respond. What will he say and what did you do to prepare the bank manager for this conversation?

Next steps

A crisis provides the chance for you as manager to become a business leader. A recovery plan requires change to be delivered quickly and with a consideration for the many conflicting stakeholder positions. This means there will be many opportunities for you to demonstrate your capabilities and potential as a leader.

To succeed in such an environment requires you to approach the challenge with fresh perspectives on your own leadership capabilities. The purpose of this book is to help you develop some of those fresh perspectives, the 'something extra', as we look at the five areas of leadership expertise that could help you build a successful recovery plan after a crisis:

> *Making the right promises.* Understand how and to whom you should make promises in the recovery plan.
> *Gathering multiple new viewpoints.* Check that you have a broad enough picture of the problems to be able to find the solutions.
> *Core business skills.* Develop new areas of competence or brush up old skills which will help build a better recovery plan.
> *Delivering results through relationships.* Discover how you could spend your time most effectively to deliver the results promised.
> *Rebuilding trust with authentic communication.* Use the resources you spend communicating the plan to best effect.

But before looking at how you can design and deliver an effective recovery plan we should look at what a business crisis is; the drivers that cause it and how to prevent one happening in the first place.

The next three chapters focus on the causes of a crisis and, most importantly, how you could prevent one.

2 What is a crisis?

The two objectives of this book are to help you identify the potential drivers of a crisis so that, as a leader, you can take action to avoid one and build a successful recovery plan after a crisis has struck. Over the next three chapters we will focus on what a crisis is and its external and internal causes. From Chapter 5 onwards we will consider how to build and implement a recovery plan.

What do we mean by crisis?

The first point is to define what we mean in this book by a crisis. This is important because failing to recognize that you have a crisis will prevent you and the rest of your management team from starting to take the actions necessary to manage and recover from it. A dictionary definition would say that a crisis is a time of intense difficulty or danger. In medical terms a crisis is the turning point of a disease, when it becomes clear whether the patient will recover or not. The origin of the word crisis is from the Greek *krisis*, meaning 'decision'. In order to produce a practical business definition of a crisis we will focus on two parts of these different definitions: the concept of a turning point and the danger the problem poses.

The working definition of a crisis that we will use is when a key stakeholder changes their view on an important assumption they are making about your business; or when you as a business fail to deliver on one of your promises.

Triggers of a crisis

Using this definition provides us with a way to start to identify the risks within your business that could trigger a crisis. The first steps to take are:

- Identify the key stakeholders.
- List the critical assumptions made by each stakeholder.
- List the promises made by the business to each stakeholder.
- Consider the danger caused by a change in any assumption and/or any broken promise.

In Chapter 1, we discussed the idea that a key role of a leader is in making, balancing and delivering on promises to various stakeholders. We described four key stakeholder groups – customers and consumers, investors and lenders, employees and suppliers. At any one time the promises between these four groups will be unbalanced and the job of a manager is to continually make adjustments to try to restore more balance. Over the medium term it is essential that all of these stakeholders are receiving value from what the business is promising and delivering. Customers have to be content with the value proposition they are receiving, investors require a return in the form of dividends and share price growth, lenders need to be paid principal and interest, employees need to be incentivized and motivated and suppliers have to earn a reasonable return and be paid.

The first stage in completing the steps above is to agree who the key stakeholders are within your business. While political correctness may prompt you to list a large number of interested parties, I urge you to focus on the top five or six. Remember that part of the value of understanding such a task is the debate that you have with your colleagues. Involving more diverse views from across the whole spectrum of your organization and its partners may flush out a stakeholder that you had not considered important before. A generic list might include investors, lenders, creditors, customers, employees, suppliers and regulators.

The next step in defining what could trigger a crisis is to list the critical assumptions that each important stakeholder is making. At any one time each of your stakeholders will have made certain assumptions about the future (market share growth, product value, reliability, future dividend growth, cash flow generation etc) based on their view of what is likely to happen in the future. These assumptions will not be the same between (or even within) each group of stakeholders. Some investors might assume that sales will grow at 3 per cent per annum, others at 6 per cent, whilst management are assuming 5 per cent. Each individual stakeholder will make regular adjustments to their assumptions about the future and take decisions such as buying or selling shares based on those revised adjustments.

Examples of other types of assumptions that different stakeholders might make are summarized in Table 2.1.

Table 2.1 Stakeholder assumptions

Stakeholder	Example Assumptions
Investors	management are trustworthy
	dividend levels will not fall next year
Lenders	free cash flow will cover interest payments
	asset values are fairly stated
Customers	product is manufactured in a responsible way
	the service is delivered by qualified people
Employees	promotion is based on merit
	our leaders have a strategy for the business
Suppliers	I will be paid
	I will have access to credit insurance

As before, part of the value of the exercise is to bring together a diverse group of people to talk about the assumptions and to record all of those assumptions in a single document.

The third step of the process is to identify and list the important promises that have been made to each stakeholder. It is necessary to distinguish between assumptions and promises. Assumptions are made by a stakeholder about your company, sector or the total economy. Whilst management will have an influence on assumptions that stakeholders make, at the end of the day the assumptions are not made by you as a manager. In contrast, a promise to a stakeholder is made by a manager. Whether it is believed or not is a decision for the stakeholder.

Table 2.2 gives some simple examples of the promises that managers make to stakeholders.

Why is all this important? A crisis for your company will more than likely destroy substantial value for everybody involved. Trying to understand the drivers of a potential crisis should help you either avoid it entirely or at least be better prepared for it. The unfortunate part is that to reap the rewards of avoiding

Table 2.2 Promises to stakeholders

Stakeholder	Example Promises
Investors	earnings will be in line with last year
	capital spending will grow with sales
Lenders	interest cover will be five times operating income
	loan repayments will be made as agreed
Customers	you cannot buy cheaper
	our products are the best quality available
Suppliers	we pay 30 days after receiving your invoice
	we do not sell your products on to the grey market

a crisis you have to invest some time and energy in analysing what could drive it to happen.

Let us return to assumptions and promises. The steps so far have required you to identify the key stakeholders, the critical assumptions they have made and the important promises you have made to them. The last step is to consider the consequences of a change in other people's assumptions and/or the breaking of promises made by the business.

Let us start with assumptions and use the retail sector as an example. The working capital and cash flow cycle of most retailers is quite simple and usually advantageous to the retailer. A customer walks into Wal-Mart, Carrefour, Tesco or Auchan, selects goods, wheels the trolley to the till and pays with cash or card. The retailer receives that cash into their bank account the same day or maybe the next. The retailer, though, does not pay their suppliers for maybe 30, 60, 90 or more days after the goods have already been sold to the customer.

The person bearing the pain of this cash flow model is clearly the supplier, who may have had to pay for their own raw materials long before the retailer pays them. To make this situation work many suppliers rely on the provision of a form of credit insurance in case the retailer fails to pay them, especially when the retailer they are supplying is not a blue chip company. In fact, given how long it takes for them to be paid, very many suppliers would consider it foolish to supply goods without this credit insurance. Therefore, if you are running a retail business one of your key stakeholders will be somebody you do not do business with at all – the big credit insurance companies such as Euler Hermes, Atradius and Coface providing the credit insurance to your suppliers. For a retail business facing a liquidity crisis the trigger points will often be either the rent payment due to landlords or the withdrawal of credit insurance for its suppliers.

What is the danger level posed by a withdrawal of credit insurance? Suppliers will demand cash on delivery or cash in advance or refuse to supply further goods. At best you have a cash hole to fill of, say, 60 days of purchases or empty shelves. At worst, you have both. Whilst the CFO of a troubled furniture retail business, I worried more about the credit insurers for my suppliers than almost any other financial creditor. Why? The landlords and banks had a vested interest in working with us to find a solution to the crisis that we faced. The credit insurers had no direct connection to us as a business. The critical assumption was that we could and would continue to pay our suppliers. In a later chapter we will talk about cash management in a crisis. At that point we will need to refer back to this example. If you want to avoid a crisis caused by a credit insurer changing their assumptions about how able or likely you are to pay your suppliers, then how you go about stretching payment terms to suppliers to generate extra cash flow is an interesting dilemma.

Let us try some more examples to illustrate our process for analysing the potential triggers of a crisis. The analysis using stakeholders, assumptions, promises and danger level is quite involved and may even be a deliberately harsh definition of an impending crisis. It is harsh because it may raise the alarm bells on an impending crisis earlier than you think is necessary. But a harsh definition is more likely to alert you earlier to the problems and possibly prevent them becoming a full blown crisis. The *Titanic* sank for many reasons but part of the cause of management complacency at the White Star Line was the assumption that the ship was unsinkable.

The most obvious recent example of a major crisis is the turmoil in the finance and banking sectors in 2008 and 2009. Imagine going back to 2005 and you are the head of a bank with a simple business model. You lend money to customers to buy their houses and you pay interest to people who you borrow the money from – either savers or institutional funders, such as other banks, investors and pension funds. What are the promises that you are balancing between the four stakeholder groups that we have identified and what are the assumptions that these groups are making about the future?

From your investors there was pressure to deliver higher levels of returns via dividends and share growth. From institutional lenders there was tremendous pressure to increase the amount that you would borrow to finance advances to customers as such lending by the institutions raised fees and income that they could use to satisfy the demands of their own investors. Never had so much money been forced upon you to lend to your new and existing customers. Investor demand for growth in profits was placing extreme pressure on you to deliver ever higher levels of new business from your customers.

In the market for your products there was, however, intense competition for new customers as everybody else had access to the same wall of money and was trying to lend it out to the same population of households. To attract and retain customers the promises that you made about lending and credit terms, pricing and service had to be competitive. In practical terms if you wanted to continue to grow your business you had to lend to people with lower credit quality and into growth segments such as buy-to-let landlords and speculative development.

Even though you relaxed the criteria for credit, to win and retain customers required that you placed ever greater sales targets upon your employees and incentivized them to deliver those targets, costing you more money in bonuses.

So now you are standing on the wobble board that we described in Chapter 1 and trying to work out what to do. What choices did you have back in 2005? Wholesale markets for lending were booming and property prices were still rising sharply. Not taking full advantage of this new economic miracle would incur the wrath of your shareholders and probably lose you your job. The media were hailing the end of boom and bust cyclical markets and the globalization of capital markets and trade was escalating.

One route at that time (2005) was to try to satisfy the demands of investors. To grow more profits and dividends required more lending to customers. To finance this growth you could increase savings deposits from households and/or increase the amount of money that you borrowed from institutions, so-called wholesale borrowings. At the time it was easier, quicker and cheaper to borrow from the wholesale markets. To use all this extra finance you needed to change your credit qualification criteria and start to include more sub-prime lending, bigger mortgages, buy-to-let landlords and commercial property developers. You also needed to change the culture in your organization to focus more on sales than credit risk.

To choose this route you and your key stakeholders had to make two critical assumptions. First, that access to wholesale funding would remain open. In 2005 this was an assumption made without too much consideration. Second, that the ever increasing value of domestic and commercial property would cover any losses from the default of the riskier borrowers that you were lending to.

Were there any signs that could have alerted you to the impending crisis? The benefit of hindsight is marvellous but let us see what might just have indicated a potential crisis. Our definition of a crisis is the turning point at which either or both of two things could happen: 1) stakeholders stop believing that their assumptions about the future are valid; 2) there is a real danger that the promises that were made to stakeholders will no longer be fulfilled.

The assumption made in this case in 2005 was that more and more money could be borrowed and lent on to households to finance property purchases without significant default risk. Was this a reasonable assumption from a customer and wholesale lender perspective? Whilst the answer to this question is now obvious and somewhat academic, why was it not so obvious back in 2005? One answer might be that the question was never asked or taken sufficiently seriously. Another might be in the word that I have repeated continuously in this chapter, 'assumption'. We all have to make assumptions about the future in order to make and balance promises to stakeholders. My personal view is that a lack of respect for assumptions is one of the prime causes of a crisis. Look in to the word – 'assume' too lightly and it can make an 'ass' of 'u' and 'me'. Two extra points to note. First, doubts about the validity of the underlying assumptions supporting a market such as wholesale funding always being available, property prices continuing to rise, are contagious and will spread very, very quickly. In fact they will spread far more quickly than management can react – changing an opinion on an assumption takes much less time than selling a portfolio of asset-backed securities. Second, once the market opinion on a core assumption has changed, people will take swift and protective actions that can often worsen the crisis. Banks stop lending to banks, so some banks go bust, causing banks to be even more reluctant to provide wholesale funding.

Some managers at banks and investors made different assumptions about the future of property lending. Some hedge funds took the view that the promises of cheap and easy credit for households would eventually cause the wholesale lenders to financial institutions to remove funding so savers might fear that the ultimate but always unsaid promise that their money was safe, was not as rock solid as they had been led to believe. A friend of mine at the head of one of these boring banks also took a different view – he gathered as much savings deposits as he could attract, bought no securitized assets and only lent to households with good credit ratings. His bank was not as glamorous as others over the years before the credit crunch, but he still has his job and his bank is secure and vibrant.

On a practical basis you and your senior team could put together a one page summary of the key assumptions and promises that you have made to your stakeholders. This has the advantage of putting the assumptions into focus and should encourage some more challenging debate about their validity. A very simplified example going back to the boring bank in 2005 might have looked something like Table 2.3.

Table 2.3 2005 banking example

Trigger	Data
Identify key stakeholders	eg wholesale lenders to my bank
List critical assumptions by stakeholder	eg additional risk of the bank's sub-prime lending is covered by increasing property values
Important promises made to each stakeholder	eg our sales staff carry out appropriate credit procedures before lending to a customer
Danger caused by changed assumption/broken promise	eg withdrawal of short dated wholesale funding will create a cash crisis at my bank

Can you construct a similar summary for your business today? Are any of the assumptions made by the stakeholders subject to significant risk of change? How would a change in the assumptions that a stakeholder made impact your business? Is there a potential for a crisis from the consequences of a change in assumptions?

Because of an IT fault, a leading global retailer lost its checkout systems at over 60 stores which were forced to shut for the day. This was a problem that required serious management response and a review of project risk management policies. However, it was not significant enough to make any of the key stakeholders change their assumptions about profit or cash generation in the context of the whole group. A problem certainly but not, in our definition, a crisis.

Preventing a crisis

The definition of a crisis that we have used provides a way to think about the potential drivers of a crisis. In the next two chapters we will look at some of the external and internal causes and drivers of a business crisis. This can be important in the work you do as a leader to prevent and in the actions you take to build a recovery plan after, a crisis.

3 External causes of a crisis

Our working definition of a crisis is the turning point when assumptions about the future change and/or there is a real danger that the promises you have made will no longer be delivered. If we follow this definition it provides us with a new way of identifying the cause of a crisis and hopefully preventing a problem turning into a crisis. We can examine a crisis by looking at the underlying assumptions and promises that a business has made and seeing what caused stakeholders to change their opinion on those assumptions and promises. To start with we can split the turning points into those primarily driven by external factors and those resulting from how the business is managed.

The four external factors we will consider are:

- Economic cycles. Consumers and companies reduce or delay spending as unemployment and recessionary pressures impact the whole economy.

- Customer priorities. A sudden change in how and with whom customers choose to prioritise their spending that can affect an individual company or a whole sector.
- Product, technology and business model innovation. An existing or new competitor changes the competitive landscape of a sector or product category.
- Outside intervention. A regulator, government or legislator changes the rules of business for a specific company, a sector or the economy as a whole.

From an internal management perspective the four causes of a turning point that we will consider in the next chapter are:

- Broken promises. Investors, lenders, customers, suppliers or employees stop wanting to invest their money or time in a company that has disappointed them.
- Corporate breakdown. Something in the company's operating system breaks down. This might be a product failure or recall, factory fire, unfavourable litigation or management scandal.
- Management optimism. Managers make over optimistic assumptions about the future and are unable or unwilling to consider a downside scenario.
- Lack of sensitivity. Leaders and managers think they are sensitive to changes in the market but miss critical trends and changes.

For each potential driver it is important to consider the root cause of the problems you are facing as this will provide some context for your recovery plan. However, identifying a single dominant cause is often hard to achieve and could also make the problem worse by focusing attention in the recovery on the wrong place. You should make the time to consider the causes of the crisis from a number of different viewpoints and consider how they interact. Set out below are some thoughts under each of the categories which we will use to stimulate your thinking about a potential crisis.

The classic example of a crisis creating a disaster is the sinking of the *Titanic*. If we ask people what caused the sinking the obvious answer is that the ship hit an iceberg and the captain was in a large way responsible for the disaster. However, there were numerous factors that contributed to the sinking. Environmental factors included a new moon which made visibility poor, a lack of wind reducing the size of waves crashing onto the icebergs and very low temperatures causing icebergs to be found further south than normal. Construction factors included brittle rather than 'bendy' steel and the poor quality of the rivets used. Human factors included the objectives and reputation of the owners and captain. For a forensic discussion of the causes of the sinking you can refer to McCarty and Foecke (2008) *What Really Sank the Titanic*.

The point to consider here is that the people involved with the *Titanic* all wanted it to be a success and did not plan to create a disaster. In fact, each of those involved was probably trying their very best to make the ship a success. As in business, very few workers and managers are trying to create a crisis. Most often they are seeking to do their own jobs well and yet there are still and always will be business disasters. To understand the cause of a crisis, and the opportunities to recover, leaders must understand the whole picture, including some things that sit on the periphery of their vision. We will first look at the four external factors which can cause a stakeholder to change their critical assumptions about the future of a business and trigger a crisis.

Economic cycles

The first external driver to consider is the health of the general economy. The markets in both developed and emerging countries have been subject to significantly higher levels of contraction and uncertainty since 2007 than in previous decades. Many of the major global markets have been in technical recession and growth in emerging markets has significantly slowed. Consumers and enterprises have been impacted by fluctuations in input costs such as fuel, commodities and foodstuffs. Despite reductions in central bank interest rates, credit became more expensive, less available and more volatile to predict. Asset values for housing, equities and pension schemes retreated significantly.

Before the recession happened what were the assumptions that key stakeholders were making about business and the economy? Two of the most important ones that were shared by almost all stakeholders were that GDP and asset values would continue to grow and that finance would be continually available to fund such growth. Put another way, increasing demand could be financed by cheap debt that allowed investors to earn higher levels of return. In such circumstances management teams changed the balance of their promises to reward investors with special dividends and share buybacks, financed by debt. The promise to the debt providers for all this extra money would be kept by generating greater cash profits from the increase in the value and volume of sales to customers and consumers. The extra, cheap finance allowed households to feel more confident about borrowing and spending. Employees and suppliers were both sharing in the spoils of never-ending economic growth and cheaper and more freely available finance. This should sound like a perfectly balanced and enjoyable management situation. We were all masters of balancing on our gold-plated, asset-backed, securitized wobble board.

So where were the signs that in fact the equation was unbalanced and assumptions about the future were about to change so rapidly we would face a crisis that threatened the entire global financial system? Whilst there are many interlinked reasons for the credit crunch crisis, as there were for the sinking of the *Titanic*, may I be bold enough to suggest that the key assumptions supporting the rapid growth in lending and household spending were not openly articulated or robustly challenged? What could have been some of those assumptions? Perhaps a key assumption was that the bank debt I borrow today to fund my leveraged buyout/share buy-back/new home, I will be able to refinance when the debt comes up for renewal. All debt has to be refinanced at some point in the future and we have to make assumptions about the availability of credit, its terms and pricing at that future date. The history of economic cycles tends to suggest that those terms can change quite significantly over the course of a few years, or even days. If I chose to borrow money over short periods of time to finance a longer-term investment in an asset that was far less liquid than my debt, then I would be even more at risk to changes in circumstances. That is why some banks and institutions which bought long-term assets like mortgage securities with short-term wholesale funding ended up in collapse.

What can any of this experience tell us about managing the risk of a crisis due to economic cycles beyond our own management control? Back to the assumptions that we make, perhaps we can challenge our plans with the following assumptions:

- Economic cycles are always with us and there will never be an end to the ups and downs.
- Debt always has to be refinanced and lenders react quickly and aggressively to the fear of a downturn.
- We may only be able to refinance on worse terms than on the finance we are just about to borrow.
- Funding assets that might be hard to turn into cash quickly with finance that has to be renewed in the short or medium term puts us at risk to general economic sentiment that is beyond our control.

I know these things are easy to say now. At the time the pressure to keep on dancing whilst the sweet music is playing is intense.

In fact you might lose your job or bonus through being seen as a party pooper by your colleagues and investors. I think that this is maybe where some of the lessons of the recent recession and crisis can be learned. Managers and leaders need to be more skilful and robust in challenging accepted wisdom and questioning the demands of their stakeholders, however unpopular that may make them. This will require executive management to be bolder in defending the balance of promises that they make and non-executive directors more vocal in their support of such decisions.

In the short term, the continuing impacts of the global credit crunch are likely to mean that:

- Access to credit will remain expensive and volatile, for both consumers and enterprises.
- Shrinking capital at banks, and a reduced risk appetite amongst creditors and credit insurers, will require all companies, not just the distressed, to produce more of their cash requirements internally.
- Negative press sentiment, falling asset values, volatility in household bills and the fear of unemployment are likely to make consumers more risk averse and increasingly price conscious.
- Enterprises will look to reduce their cost bases in order to protect margins and to lower prices to maintain or grow volumes.

There are probably as many views as there are economists about how long and how deep any recession or downturn and its aftermath might be. For a business leader, trying to predict the timing of a downturn is not necessarily the best use of their time. Perhaps the old maxim of 'hope for the best but plan for the worst' is a useful motto for managers. In Chapters 7 and 8 we will consider some of the core business skills that may help you manage through and beyond a recession or downturn.

In summary, do not assume that today's economic circumstances will continue forever when things are good, or get better quickly when the economy is bad. Whatever the circumstances, you will be at a competitive advantage if you generate more of your cash flow needs from internal sources.

Customer priorities

The second possible external cause of a crisis relates to the spending intentions of customers and consumers. To be clear, such changes in the normal course of competitive business should not be an external factor that causes a crisis. If it does become a crisis this is because management has been insensitive to the changes in the market that have been happening and have failed to react to them. We will discuss this further below when we look at management's lack of sensitivity. The factor we are looking at here is the risk of a sudden change in spending patterns that it would be much harder for a management team to predict. Hence this factor may be more of an outlying risk of causing a crisis but it can have a dramatic impact if it occurs. This is also not about the issues of product safety failure that we will consider under the category of corporate breakdowns.

So what are these infrequent but risky causes of a crisis? The obvious first answer is related to the category of economic cycles discussed above. A change in consumer sentiment about their wealth and continuing employment can cause rapid changes in spending decisions that last for many years. For example, a key strategic priority of consumer packaged goods companies in recent years has been the move towards premium products. In food, coffee, alcoholic drinks and personal care the global companies have been offering consumers superior versions of their products. A triple-filtered vodka drink does not cost much more to produce than a double-filtered vodka.

However, the right packaging, brand activation and advertising can drive consumers to pay a significant price premium for the triple filtered product. This creates margin expansion possibilities that for the last decade have been the dream of consumer product companies, dreams that have been very effectively realized by many, with both consumers and investors pleased with the results. In a recession such a strategy can have mixed outcomes. Some premium products see an uptake in demand as households start to feel the pinch. While it used to be the premium lipsticks that sold better during a downturn it seems in the latest recession that foundation make-up has been the luxury product winner for women. Trading down by consumers can lead some companies struggling to ensure that they have the right price points, package sizing and brand image for the now more cost conscious customer. And in more expensive goods, be they kitchens, cars or wide-bodied aircraft, the effect can be much more pronounced.

What can be done proactively to prepare for or even prevent a crisis relating to such changes in customer spending? Part of the preparation is related to what we discussed in the context of economic cycles – never assume that the cycle of boom and bust has come to a permanent end. As you pursue a product strategy that capitalizes on consumers' willingness to spend more on premium products, it is important to ensure that you have a portfolio of products that allows consumers to trade down as fast and conveniently as you encouraged them to trade up. Since 2009 Nestlé has been benefiting from its Popularly Positioned Product strategy, which offers lower income households relevant and nutritional products at affordable prices, in both its emerging and developed markets.

The other way to stay prepared for any of the sudden changes in spending that we will discuss is to maintain cost control, even when times are booming. This is a theme that we will return to throughout the book and in particular in Chapter 8. A London

Business School case study (Sull and Escobari, 2005) quotes Marcel Telles, the then Chairman and CEO of the Brazilian brewer Companhia Cervejaria Brahma, now Anheuser Busch InBev, precisely on this point:

> Efficiency and low costs are the best insurance you can have in a turbulent environment. We always say that when the storm comes and everyone else is drowning, we want to hold our breath longer. If everyone else drowns in three minutes, we want to be able to survive two minutes longer. Operational efficiency lets you do that. We have to hammer and hammer on cost savings and efficiency all the time. Sometimes when the business is going great, people start looking at you and ask why are we pushing for so much hardship? The answer is simple. This is our insurance for unexpected things in really hard times.

A second area where sudden changes in customer spending patterns may arise is related to changes in consumers' perceptions of risk. As we discussed in Chapter 1, certain industries are very susceptible to rapid changes in consumers' expectations and evaluation of risk. The outbreak or likelihood of any version of avian, swine or other type of pandemic flu virus can hit companies' income lines very hard and very fast. Terrorist actions committed or threatened can also cause immediate and dramatic reductions in customer spending. Unfortunately, it seems that the companies whose business models require some of the largest investments in fixed assets are also those that are most susceptible to short-term changes in customer spending habits. Even in a recession or time of political crisis, consumers will still make mobile telephone calls, surf the internet, shop for groceries and drink alcohol, even though it might be less of a premium brand. However, putting off a flight or hotel visit can be done quickly and often without any penalty. The trouble is that the airline or hotel operator still has to pay the costs of their significant fixed asset bases – aircraft, booking systems, maintenance, properties and staff. If you are in an industry that can be subject to large, rapid swings in customer spending what actions can you take to prevent a loss of revenue becoming a liquidity crisis? In Chapters 7 and 8 we will discuss the issues of maintaining sales, cost base restructuring and cash flow management. At this point we can consider the question of operational versus financial leverage.

One of the lessons from the most recent recession is that high levels of financial leverage can produce super levels of returns for shareholders in the good times and bankruptcy in the bad times. Financial leverage is the amount of debt that I have borrowed to finance my business or household spending. For example, if I buy a house for $300,000 and borrow 90 per cent of the purchase price, I will owe my mortgage provider $270,000. If house prices go up 8 per cent per annum for three years, then my house will be worth over $375,000 after only 36 months. At an interest rate of 5 per cent on the mortgage borrowings of $270,000 I have had to pay $40,500 for the mortgage interest over three years. The net result would be a very healthy 115 per cent return on an initial investment of $30,000, for very little work. In these circumstances the more money I can borrow the less of my own money I have to use and the bigger percentage return I will earn on my investment. Conversely, a 5 per cent annual reduction in house prices over three years will mean that my property will be worth less than $260,000. I will still have to pay the bank interest of $40,500 (as whatever happens the bank will still want to be paid) and now I'll be sitting on a total loss of over $80,000. The consequences of this on households have been seen across the world in the last few years.

Operational leverage reflects how a change in output, for our purposes, sales, impacts bottom line profitability. Specifically, in assessing the robustness of your business to a sudden decline in demand, how far and how fast can you avoid both variable and fixed costs to compensate for a loss of income? The answer to this question is twofold. How low is your break even and how fast can you lower it?

By preparing some scenarios of different levels of demand, including volume, mix and pricing, you can create three or four calculations of your break even position under different levels of crisis or distress. From this you can explore actions that could be taken to lower the break even level even further and understand what is the lowest level of demand you could survive without suffering severe financial distress. This should provide two insights. First, as a management team do we truly understand how costs, cash flow and profits flex with changing levels and type of demand? Second, given a better understanding of our operational leverage what is our attitude to using financial leverage to boost returns to investors?

Intelligence in this area is clearly related to the issue of management sensitivity, which we will touch on later. If asked to look into the crystal ball of potential drivers of rapid and significant changes in customer spending habits I might venture that consumer perceptions of water usage by large food and beverage organizations, energy consumption and the joys of thrift might be some areas to think about. Maybe post-Lehman Brothers I will drink tap water rather than bottled Fijian water, drive a smaller car and decide that an American Express green card is a cooler colour than gold, platinum or black. These are all decisions that can be taken quickly by me, the consumer, but which can have, if enough people do the same, significant consequences for businesses.

Product, technology and business model innovation

The third area of external change that could generate a crisis is in the area of innovation. As with potential changes to customer spending priorities, the normal cut and thrust of competition will produce a continuous flow of innovations that managers have to anticipate, be sensitive to and responsive to. This normal level of innovation is something that a leader should expect to have to manage and on its own is not a driver of crisis. Failure to respond to market innovation will create a crisis if management is too optimistic in its assumptions or insensitive to what is changing. However, in this third area of external drivers we are considering a level of innovation which is outside the normal and much harder to predict or plan for. As we have already seen, things that are harder to predict will always have a greater potential to create a crisis and often require a different approach to management and leadership. As with our discussions about all of the drivers of a potential crisis, the objective of this section, like the previous ones, is to make you think more broadly about your own business and the markets it operates in so you can identify the factors on the periphery of your vision that might pose a danger.

On that basis, what types of innovation should we be worrying about? When many people talk about innovation the first thing that comes to mind is product changes. When we talk about product changes we inevitably end up talking about Apple. If you had been a manufacturer of mobile handsets, particularly in the growing smartphone segment, how could you have known that the iPhone would take a 10 per cent worldwide market share in a couple of years? When I talked to a director of one of the major handset manufacturers he told me that the technology that goes into the iPhone had been available for a long time. But the industry had been so busy competing in the same way they always had with their traditional competitors that they missed the point of real product innovation. He now regrets that they were focused on adding another megapixel to the definition of the camera on the phone as a way of competing rather than taking a wider view of innovation and the customer. As with many of the other things that we talk about in this book, if you want to avoid a crisis in the first place you have to take time to step back and think creatively about your business and its markets. You will not avoid an impending crisis just by being excellent at execution.

This starts to lead us to some techniques for thinking about innovation and spotting trends that have the potential to generate a crisis for you. Before we move away from Apple there is one other thought we should consider. In the creation of both the iPod and the iPhone, Apple innovated not just in terms of the product but also in terms of a total customer solution. The innovation was not the iPod but the iPod plus iTunes. The innovation was not the iPhone but the iPhone plus the App Store. Both inventions made it easy for customers to achieve what they wanted via a seamless integration of hardware and content. Apple was taking a more holistic view of the business they were in, not just looking to create the greatest megapixel camera known to man. This type of approach can be described as 'systems thinking'.

Systems thinking is a philosophy, or approach to problem solving, that encourages us to understand the whole rather than the individual parts of an issue. A few years ago I spent the day with Russell Ackoff at Wharton Business School. Ackoff is one of the architects of systems thinking. The piece that really struck home in relation to systems thinking and innovation was the need to take both the bigger picture and to understand how things actually worked in practice at shop or factory floor level. To identify potential innovations at a product, technology or system-wide level will require you to do two things. First, to consider your business in the widest possible context of customers' needs and desires – I like to call this the 'top of the mountain' view. Second, to spend time at different, ground floor, points in the market and in your business to see what is happening at the coalface.

We can use a couple of examples to illustrate the actions that need to be taken to try to avoid an innovation becoming a crisis for you. To start with we will consider the top of the mountain approach to identifying potential innovations that might have an adverse impact on your position in the market. My very first job was making and serving ice creams at a boating holiday resort. The machine I operated was a wonderful piece of Italian engineering, manufactured by a company called Carpigiani. The setup in the morning required time, patience and lots of sterilizing solution; it really was a labour of love. The first cone of the day that was produced by freezing the liquid ice-cream mixture was the richest and best. The gross margins for the store owner were excellent. The drawbacks were that we could use only one flavour at a time, when it was busy customers had to wait while the liquid froze and if it rained we ended up throwing away a lot of unsold ice cream. In addition, the machines were relatively expensive and required servicing as well as loving. From a customer perspective we provided a choice of one flavour, many different sizes, with the necessary chocolate flake in the top. On sunny days there were very long queues.

The question is how could you compete with Carpigiani and its soft ice-cream machines? If you took the approach of one of the big mobile phone handset manufacturers you might focus on making a better machine, one that freezes more quickly, has multiple flavours or uses less electricity. However, if you were Apple entering this market how might you approach the opportunity? How about dispensing with the machine altogether? There are many ice-cream outlets that serve frozen ice-cream lollies and scoops of ice cream from tubs. These outlets do not have to clean and set up a machine each morning, can offer multiple flavours and have a lower stock wastage risk if it is raining. However, there is still something attractive to consumers about a soft ice cream, prepared in front of them and with a chocolate flake in the top. How could you serve this market without the hassle and expense of providing a $6,000 machine?

Unilever provided the answer in 2002. It introduced a manual machine that used one-shot packages of multi-flavour soft ice creams which were dispensed into a cone. Was it as romantic and theatrical as a Carpigiani machine? Did the vanilla taste as good as the real thing from the Italian maker? Probably not. For a street vendor, however, they had a low cost, low maintenance, high brand awareness way of selling soft ice creams. For consumers they had an increased access to soft ice creams in situations when they would not have been available before. In addition, they had a wider choice of flavours. The innovation was not about making a better ice-cream machine; it was about fulfilling the needs of the street vendors and consumers with a different business model. The question you should ask and answer is how would you compete with yourself if you were not constrained by the way that you currently do business?

A second way to explore the dangers to your business model of potential innovation is by walking about at the ground floor level in your market and business. The Japanese have a term for this: *gemba*. Based on the kanji characters for gemba, it literally means 'what the king sees'. In business, this translates into walking around inside and outside your business to understand what is happening at the coalface.

In order to obtain real insight from the time you spend walking around you need to be in the right frame of mind. It is an incredibly valuable use of your walking around time to seek incremental improvements in the operation of your business. It is also good to listen and learn what the morale is like at the front line. However, some of your visits should be focused solely on thinking about how somebody else could innovate you into a crisis. If innovation is held up as the saviour of companies, the converse is also true. Let me repeat this: if innovation is your strategic life saver then somebody else's innovation might be your death sentence. If you are the victim of somebody else's successful innovation then your next crisis is likely to be just round the corner. Contrast how much time you spend fostering innovation in your company with being paranoid about what everybody else is working on. A healthy paranoia can be a good thing, because, in truth, everybody *is* out there trying to destroy your business and livelihood. Paranoia can help you get in the right frame of mind for taking some shop floor tours. In a paranoid state what might we see if we took a tour of your business and market?

Outside intervention

The last driver of a potential crisis from an external perspective is when a regulator, government or legislator changes the rules of the game for a specific company, a sector or the economy as a whole. These types of changes can result in sudden and cataclysmic impacts that have terminal consequences for a company. Why? Because a critical stakeholder has removed a company's licence to operate or ability to trade profitably and management has very little time or few ways to respond. This is a perfect crisis that management did not see coming and its impact on value can be enormous.

Are all of these types of change so unpredictable? Obviously not, as many of the trends that result in changes in rules and regulation take a long time to have an impact that creates a crisis. Part of the definition of a crisis that we have been using is to consider the turning point when a stakeholder changes a critical assumption that has a dangerous impact on your business. We have discussed the need to try to seek a continual re-balancing of the promises that you make to key stakeholders, customers, investors, people and suppliers. In this section I want to consider a way of identifying those trends that might lead to a turning point in regulatory or government assumptions. The essential question is to ask what are the formal and informal 'licences' that are granted to your business to operate as it does? Governments, regulators and local authorities act as 'suppliers' of these formal and informal licences and in doing so certain assumptions are made about your business, the market and wider society.

The first area to consider is in relation to customers and consumers. Table 3.1 shows a series of categories and questions for you to consider in identifying risk areas. Read the first column first.

Table 3.1 Risk areas in relation to customers and consumers

Category of Customer 'Licence'	Key Questions
1. Formal licences, eg consumer credit registration, health and safety regulations, financial bonding requirements, industry approvals (eg in aviation) 2. Informal licences, eg advertising standards, anti-competition laws 3. Social licences, eg degree of tolerance of harmful products and services	a. As senior management do we have a complete list of all the formal, informal and social licences that apply to our business and our customers? b. What could change within our business to put us in breach of the requirements of a licence? c. What are the key assumptions that the providers of the licence are making when drawing up the rules? d. What would need to happen for one of those assumptions to change? e. How adaptive is our business model to comply with revised regulations resulting from a change in assumptions?

We have used three categories of licence to think about the potential areas of risk. A formal licence is one that your business has to apply for and comply with the terms of its rules and regulations. If you want to be a bank then you have to register as a bank and comply with the rules of the financial authority that issues the banking licences. An informal licence is one where the business does not have to apply for a licence but must operate its business in accordance with underlying legislation or regulation. For example, there will be standards set on what you can promise to customers in many forms of media advertising, although lower standards would seem to apply to spam e-mails offering men and women an opportunity to improve their personal relationships via different coloured pills. In the last category, that of social licences, fall the less well defined 'regulations' that political, market and social norms can apply to a business. Social licences would include tolerance (or lack of) for products or services that may have a harmful or corrupting influence on consumers and the environment. Obvious industries would include tobacco, alcohol, arms and pornography. In sectors where there is a social licence provided by society for potentially harmful products or services there is clearly an increased risk of a change in assumptions removing the social licence to trade profitably. The tobacco industry has faced this change in assumptions over many years as more and more countries adopt a dark market approach, the removal of all forms of advertising and promotion and increasing taxation to reduce consumption.

Looking forward there are a number of trends that could impact sectors that have not felt the same sort of pressure from changes in social licence as has tobacco. Adjacent categories such as alcohol could come under scrutiny through the profits they make from over-consumption by a small segment of their consumers. Increasing concerns about water usage in food production could put pressure on multi-nationals as to the sustainability of their supply chains. Current accounting methods used around the world do not provide for the environmental replacement costs of how a business uses and abuses limited supplies of resources, be that energy, carbon emissions or productive land. A populist change in society's assumptions about what is acceptable or not can lead to politicians making rapid changes to the formal, informal and social licences under which businesses operate.

From the perspective of a risk of a crisis, I would assume that where your business has explicit formal or known informal licences to operate you take the time to manage the risks associated with them. Perhaps the area for most concern regarding a surprise change is in the last area of social licences. One way of digging deeper here is to look for instances where your business makes a super profit. For example, perhaps as a result of geography, distribution, supply chain control or regulation your business has established a category of customers from which it makes what others might consider excessive profits. While you may think this is the result of skilful strategy and flawless execution, others might seek to argue that the consequences of those super profits have a negative effect on society and markets. Could those profits be seen to be coming from an exploitation of obese children, alcoholics, closure of small businesses, lack of choice or the vulnerable position of the elderly or the suffering? We can all identify companies and sectors that have come under political and societal pressure from the profits they make in certain countries, markets or consumer segments. The consequences of such pressures have led to a crisis for many companies.

Within the purpose of this book, the process I would consider to avoid a potential crisis from changes in the assumptions behind a social licence is this: identify all the areas where your company makes much higher than average profits. Honestly appraise the risks that a change in social opinion or political reaction to how those profits are made could come about and how it would impact you. Consider the actions that could be taken to mitigate those risks. Then decide whether continuing to make the super profits outweighs the possibility of a potential change in assumptions creating a damaging turning point for your business.

4 Internal drivers of a crisis

We can itemize four causes arising from within management that contribute to a crisis-generating turning point. They are:

- Broken promises. Investors, lenders, customers, suppliers or employees stop wanting to invest their money or time in a company that has disappointed them.
- Corporate breakdown. Something in the company's operating system breaks down. This might be a product failure or recall, factory fire, unfavourable litigation or management scandal.
- Management optimism. Managers make over-optimistic assumptions about the future and are unable or unwilling to consider a downside scenario.
- Lack of sensitivity. Leaders and managers think that they are sensitive to movements in the market but miss critical trends and changes.

Broken promises

We have said the seeds of a crisis germinate at the point where a key stakeholder changes a critical assumption about a business and/or when an important promise made by management is broken. The purpose of this section of the book is to help you identify potential internal drivers of a crisis. Understanding what promises have been made is a good place to start. Many of the companies I have helped through a crisis did not have a complete or up to date schedule of all the critical promises the business had made to its stakeholders. The first question must be whether your business knows what promises have been made and how and when those promises are reviewed and assessed.

An easy place to consider this driver from is the promises that are made to financial stakeholders – investors and lenders. We can focus on lenders as an example of what needs to be done. When your company borrows money from a bank there is a very simple exchange of promises, although the scope, scale and complexity of the negotiations often obscure the underlying contract. Except for the largest, most creditworthy organizations, most companies will have to submit a business plan and financial forecast to support their request for funds. This forecast, or prospective financial information, will contain a series of assumptions about the future. Management will consider sales, costs, working capital, tax rates and capital spending requirements for the next three or five years. A sensitivity will be applied and a 'base case' set of projections will be submitted. This base case will, hopefully, show that the company can pay back the interest and principal that it wants to borrow from the bank. You, as management, will have applied a level of rigour to produce a realistic set of forecasts before submitting them to the bank. The important question for you is what words do you use to think about these forecasts? Companies I have advised that have run into problems with their banks when forecasts have not been achieved have often considered the plans as a set of reasonable assumptions about the future. They are surprised when their banks take a more questioning and sceptical stance to changes to those assumptions. Why?

Consider the position from the bank's point of view. They receive your business plan and forecasts, probably apply their own sensitivities to them, and then construct a response. They promise to provide money at a certain interest rate, for a defined period of time with certain conditions, for example covenant compliance and security for the borrowings. The lead banker will have to go before a credit sanctioning committee to argue the case for the company and gain approval. Remember that you as management will not be at the credit committee meeting; your relationship banker will be there arguing your case based on the forecasts that you have provided. Your assumptions about future cash flow will become the promises that you are making to the bank in exchange for their lending your company money. Whether articulated as such in the documentation or not you are making promises in exchange for money. From the bank's point of view, if they lend you the money they have assumed that those promises have been made after due care and attention and that you mean to deliver on them.

Six months down the line your view of the future has changed and actual results are not in line with the assumptions, the promises, that you made. You now start providing revised forecasts to the bank. What impact does receiving those revised forecasts have on the bank? Minor adjustments are normal. Even minor adjustments, however, if happening on a regular basis, will begin to feel to your bank as a breach of the promises that you made in order to convince them to lend you the money. Every new downward revision of the forecasts chips away at the confidence the bank has in your ability to run your business. In addition, the bank will increasingly feel that your sincerity in making the initial promises was not as great as they believed at the time. Each change in assumption following from a broken promise erodes trust in management. When, as an advisor, I hear from a bank that they no longer trust management to be able to forecast future cash flows I know we shall be in for a tough time in agreeing a way forward.

I want to be clear about something at this point. I am not advocating that you hide deteriorating conditions affecting future cash flows from your bank just to try to retain their confidence. Every banker I know would prefer to have an early insight into changes and problems because this allows them to work with the company to resolve difficult situations while there are more options on the table. What I am urging you to think about is the serious nature of assumptions, promises in the eyes of the bank, you make when raising money. Changing assumptions because of fundamental changes in the market is one thing. Changing them because you did not put enough diligence into the original plans is another. Broken promises destroy trust and generate a crisis. Take great care over the promises that you make and think about them as serious marriage vows rather than financial forecasts.

Later, in Chapters 7 and 8, we will cover some of the essential business skills to help make better promises. At this point the most important point to remember is always to ensure that you have, and are seen to have, total mastery of your cash flow management and forecasting. Dear board members, it is not enough to leave cash to your treasurer or CFO. The best preparation for any form of crisis is to show that the senior leadership in the company understands cash on an intimate basis and has taken all the actions necessary to control and forecast it. When I undertake business reviews for banks into companies in crisis the very best thing I can say to the bank is that, despite the difficulties, broken promises and market conditions, the senior leadership team really is taking cash management and forecasting extremely seriously. We will discuss what needs to be done to achieve this later in the book. One of the reasons for an emphasis on this area of cash is that it is one of the two resources that are normally in short supply in a crisis. The other is time. One of the best ways to buy more time is to demonstrate that you have cash forecasting under total control.

Many of the same points apply to promises made to investors. For the leadership of a listed company there are many events during the year when it is expected to make future promises about the business and update on promises previously made. Annual meetings, quarterly earnings reports and shareholder meetings are all essentially about current and new promises. To fully appreciate this we need to look at the very simple proposition as to why an investor owns shares in your company. Ignoring the short selling of shares for the moment, an investor makes a financial return in two ways: the dividends the company pays and a rise in the share price.

Although there are myriad ways of valuing a company, the most fundamental driver is future assumptions about cash generation. Every professional investor will have a spreadsheet model with vacant cells to be filled with assumptions about sales, costs, tax rates, working capital and capital investment. They will fill these cells with their view on the company, its market and management. A critical input into their decision as to which assumptions to make will be the results that management has delivered and what the leadership says about the future. Clearly, investors will make a range of different assumptions that will produce different valuations based on a discounted cash flow calculation. Based on that variety of valuations, different investors will decide whether to buy, hold or sell a share. This difference in view creates supply and demand for a share that determines the price on a listed company stock exchange.

Based on this, as an investor you should be watching for every piece of information that is available to refine and update your assumptions in the spreadsheet. In fact, there is a whole industry, both professional and amateur, devoted to collating, scrutinizing and opining on every scrap of data, comment and gossip about a company. One of the real eye openers for me as a CFO of a listed company was a meeting at a Swiss investment bank with one of the sector's leading analysts. Within five minutes of our first meeting he produced a schedule of all the written and spoken 'promises' that the business had made over the last 10 years. These were broken down into sections by strategy, sales, costs, products, supply chain, working capital, capital spending and dividend intentions. For each comment, or, in his words, promise, there was a meticulous and detailed record of actual performance against each line. For him this analysis provided three areas of insight: the validity or robustness of each promise in relation to what assumption he should make in his valuation model; the trustworthiness of the current management in making promises about the future, and the trustworthiness of the business itself, not the existing management, in making commitments about future strategy and execution. I am afraid that the analysis of the company I had stepped in to help did not make for comfortable reading. For our purposes the key point is that he was one of many people keeping a complete and accurate record of the promises the business was making about future performance and delivery. The other point was that as a company we did not have an internal schedule detailing the promises that we had made and the likely risk that they would not be fulfilled.

As with banks always treat what you say to investors as promises, not intentions. For one CFO that I worked with the answer was not to make any promises to investors. While this may be an excellent strategy for not being held to account, it does not prevent investors from making assumptions in their spreadsheets to determine valuations. They just make those assumptions without any management input. It may be that your company is in the happy position of not having to make any promises but in times of crisis the assumptions that investors have made without any guidance can result in a deeper problem. Once again we are on the leadership wobble board trying to determine the right balance of promises to be made. And always keep a register of the promises you make and, as importantly, investors might think you have made. As with some of the other lists I have been encouraging you to make, this requires effort, thought and a willingness to sustain and review the process and its implications. All of this extra effort goes towards the goal of identifying a potential crisis early and taking actions to avoid one.

Corporate breakdown

The second internal driver of a potential crisis is some form of corporate breakdown. Obvious examples of this include a product failure or recall, factory fire, unfavourable litigation or management scandal. Before considering any of these individually, we should ask the question whether there is any common link between the different types of corporate breakdown. If there is, then as a leader you can take actions to predict and control the possibility of a corporate breakdown from a system-wide perspective and this would be an invaluable tool for a manager. It is outside the scope of this book to look at the functional risk management procedures to deal with things such as keeping a food factory in compliance with health and safety legislation or employees from stealing critical assets. Here we want to examine the proposition that there might be some approaches to identify a range of business-wide breakdowns. I think the answer is there is no complete, single early warning system for all forms of corporate breakdown. However, I will argue that there are at least four traits of a business that a leader can monitor to help identify such breakdowns from a system-wide perspective. In this section we will look at two of them: first, management lacking a sufficiently detailed 360 degree view of the business and second, unbalanced economics and incentivization. The other two, management optimism and lack of sensitivity, will be dealt with in separate sections below. The four traits are:

- No 360 degree view. Decisions are made at a board room level without a genuine understanding of how the business actually operates.
- Unbalanced economics and incentivization. A business model, product or promise that works in the short term but is a ticking time bomb which remuneration policies obscure until too late.
- Management optimism. Leaders always assuming that things will be better than they turn out to be and responding too late to adversity.
- Lack of sensitivity. Managers do not scan their environment, market and business effectively enough to pick up on emerging trends and threats.

My suggestion is that devoting some serious management effort to these four areas can make a worthwhile impact on the incidence of serious corporate breakdowns. They will not, unfortunately, eradicate the possibility entirely. A business has to take risks in order to make a profit. If all risks are eliminated in order to prevent a potential breakdown or crisis then the business is unlikely to be either competitive or profitable unless it holds some form of unassailable monopoly.

We should start by examining two seemingly unrelated types of corporate breakdown: first, a serious failure of an IT system implementation and second an adverse outcome from a critical legal judgement.

A company I worked with for a number of years in the retail furniture sector considered the IT systems behind its supply chain were causing poor customer service, costing too much money and much higher levels of stock than was necessary. All of these factors provided a strong business case to improve the

IT behind the system to enable a more effective and efficient supply chain. The business model for the company was to sell kitchens and fitted bedrooms from retail showrooms and deliver the goods to customers' homes via a national and regional warehousing system. For our purpose we will focus on the home delivery of kitchens. For those of you who have ever had a new kitchen fitted you are likely to remember the trials and difficulties involved. An average, mass market kitchen consists of over 100 separate boxes supplied by as many as 40 different suppliers. A company has to bring together all of these pieces at the right time and deliver them undamaged to a customer's home. A serious logistical challenge. Also when a piece of the kitchen is missing or damaged the recovery costs can quickly eat up all of the profits from the sale of the kitchen in the costs of redelivery, of having a fitter come back on another day and compensation for the homeowner. If a supply chain and its supporting IT systems could improve the accuracy and success of the home delivery then there was a substantial opportunity for sales and profit improvement and, not least, happier customers.

When the new system was switched on it took about a week before the supply chain collapsed. Some kitchens required 10 or more home deliveries to complete an order, there was almost no stock visibility and financial performance plunged into a huge loss. As with the sinking of the *Titanic* we discussed in an earlier chapter, there was no single cause of the breakdown. Incorrect hardware and software specification and configuration, lack of involvement of the business with the IT design and a lack of clean and accurate data all played a role. The question is what could the leadership team have done to better foresee and prevent the breakdown that occurred?

I want to focus on the possession by the management of a sufficiently detailed 360 degree view of the business. I consider that one of the areas in which the company could have done better, in addition to the risk management and control of the

IT project itself, was to have had a clearer insight into the business model we were asking the IT solution to improve. A more rounded, detailed understanding of the supply chain might have changed our view on the risks and solutions required. On a system-wide view our fulfilment model was to bring together all 100 boxes needed for a customer's kitchen at the same time and deliver them, undamaged, at a time when the customer said they would be at home. In addition, we held no local stock available to recover quickly when an order had a piece missing or damaged. In a normal retail environment a store holds stock on its shelves and the customer travels to the shop to make and pay for their choices. If the shop does not have the stock required then they will leave either not having made a purchase or having made a substitute selection. The downside for the retailer is a potential lost sale. The downside for the customer is they have wasted their time and effort going to the shop and returning home unfulfilled. An unsatisfying transaction for both parties. If, however, as the retailer you have agreed to deliver a kitchen to a customer's home the economics of the story are not so simple or without deeper consequences. If the kitchen is not delivered in full and undamaged, the retailer has to return however many times is necessary to fulfil the order. In other words, the immediate economic consequences of being out of stock are radically different from those of a retailer who requires the customer to visit the store to choose and take away goods. For Ikea, the risk of an out of stock or damaged product rests with the customer. For a home delivery kitchen company the risk of an out of stock or damaged product remains with the retailer until the order is successfully completed. Such a difference in where the economic risk lies can have a devastating financial impact on a company. Where should the leadership team go to gain this insight and understand whether even a perfect IT system could solve the underlying business issues associated with home delivery? This company operated showrooms that held no stock, national and local warehouses, factories, call centres and home delivery vans. Where should a manager go to understand the business? The obvious answer is everywhere but where should the priorities and balance of time have been? Where would you go?

Senior management spent most of its time, as most management teams do, on internal planning and review meetings, stakeholder communication, board matters, investor and lender concerns, strategy insights and executive visibility. The showrooms were an essential part of the business as this was where a sale to a customer was made. Essential considerations were advertising, product development, store design and layout and staff training and incentivization. Senior business managers in a food store would be able to gain a great insight into customers and the business by stacking shelves and working on the checkout tills. For this kitchen business, however, the most important part of the customer experience was when the delivery van arrived at a customer's home. The greatest insight into the capability of the business to fulfil its promise to customers could be had at this point. The best place to gain a feeling for the strategic rationale for the operating model and effectiveness of the supply chain was by riding on a delivery van for a few days a month. This was not something the senior management prioritized. A few rides on the delivery van gave a perspective on whether the proposed new IT system, even if it were perfectly implemented, could reap the business case benefits promised. It would also question whether the way the IT project was being designed would make matters better or worse. The fact was that the flexibility of the old system allowed dedicated staff, who understood the problems of home delivering a kitchen, to devise workarounds to deliver the best customer service that was possible. The new system removed their capability to do this and that created a corporate crisis.

What am I trying to illustrate with this example? Two things. First, strategy and plans on paper in a board room cannot be effectively implemented if management do not have a granular understanding of how the business actually works. Few companies actually operate according to the procedures and structures written down as corporate belief. A boardroom is not the place to gain a detailed enough insight into your business. It is understood by almost all managers that they should spend time at the coalface of the business. I wonder, given the time pressures of running large, complex businesses, how much time is actually spent on the factory floor. In addition, when you do spend time, make sure it is from a variety of viewpoints that can provide a 360 view of the business, a subject we will return to in Chapter 6.

The second point is that a crisis waiting to happen is when you use the wrong solution to an underlying problem. Management in this case believed that an IT system could improve the home delivery supply chain to such a point that on time, in full, undamaged delivery of 100 boxes of kitchen parts could be made to such a high frequency that major financial benefits could be enjoyed. A different view would have been that such a Herculean task was not achievable. Such a view might have concluded that putting stock closer to the households that were being served allowed for a faster and cheaper recovery when the inevitable delivery problems arose. On such a basis the focus would not be on the IT system but on the fundamental assumptions underlying the supply chain. A change in the supply chain model some 10 years previously had laid the unstable foundations that led to a major crisis for the company. Twenty years ago the business had been profitable when customers had to collect the boxes that made up their kitchens from the store. The risks of out of stocks and damage resided with the consumer. When the business moved to home delivery the economics shifted so that the company bore all the risks of stock, damage and the customer not being at home when the delivery van arrived. This change caused the long-term economics of the business to alter at a fundamental level. In fact it made it structurally unprofitable unless home delivery could be executed at a level of perfection that never was the case.

From an incentives point of view the things being measured were the percentage of deliveries made on time and in full – an essential key performance indicator. However, what was not being measured was the total cost of recovery, where the major financial implications lay.

One final thought on major IT systems implementations. Much has been written about the failure of such projects and the crises that have been created for companies. The bald truth is that companies must always continue to use IT to enable better, cheaper and faster processes that can drive competitive advantage. In addition, such projects carry significant risks and millions of man hours have been devoted to identifying and managing the risks involved. Yet regular media reports still highlight the disasters that happen to companies as a result of failed IT projects. When you are implementing such programmes I am sure you will use all forms of risk management and advice to minimize the chances of failure. Can I suggest one extra form of insurance? You can use the risks of the IT project to remake senior leadership's commitment to connect with the grass roots of the business. In the business case for the project you could specifically cost in the additional time that senior managers will spend on the shop floor. In the benefits tracking process for the project, you monitor and manage how much time leaders are spending with staff on the delivery vans, production workers in the factory and accounts staff processing invoices. As with other aspects of the project, if the time being spent is not on plan this should raise a serious red flag. I have not seen many business plans for an IT project that cost in and monitor the extra time and back-fill costs that senior managers will spent at the coalface ensuring the real business needs are being addressed by the hundreds of programmers and analysts designing the IT systems. Does yours?

The second example is about a critical legal judgement that goes against a business. This could involve serious differences about customer or employee contractual rights, anti-trust situations or the interpretation of government or regulator laws and rules. We are not talking here about tactical legal moves to advance a particular strategy or objective, but the types of legal cases that have the potential to create a serious corporate breakdown and crisis.

Established in 1762, the UK-based life assurance company, Equitable Life, was seen as one of the premier institutions for professionals to select when investing their savings for a financially secure retirement. In fact, the brand was targeted at the professional middle classes. By 2000 the business was effectively bust and savers have seen their retirements blighted by the reduced returns they are now receiving. This reversal in fortunes hinged upon a legal judgement that changed the financial viability of Equitable Life and created an all consuming crisis for the company and its savers. The business was closed to new business and various parts either sold or placed into run-off. A long list of inquiries and investigations have been conducted. A very simplified version of the legal issue is that Equitable Life had guaranteed a certain level of return to some policyholders. At the time it was made this promise did not have major commercial consequences, as the promised level was lower than the actual market levels of return. However, over the years the market levels of return fell below the guaranteed amounts. Equitable Life did not have sufficient assets to pay the guaranteed amounts from the investments made for the guaranteed policyholders. The company sought to alter the amounts that would be paid to the guaranteed policyholders and the highest court in the UK ruled that they were not entitled to do so. There was not enough money put aside to pay out all of the claims of all of the various types of policyholders and almost everybody suffered as a consequence.

The underlying issue was not a legal one but a commercial one. In order to sell a certain type of retirement savings product, from the 1950s onwards until 1988, Equitable Life had made a promise to customers about the level of return they would receive. This time bomb exploded in 2000 when the courts enforced the promise as Equitable Life sought to wriggle out of its commitments. Why had the promise been made and why were the potential consequences not understood? I can only hypothesize at this point.

When I worked in a life assurance business the major concern, as with most businesses, was generating new sales. To achieve this we would juggle the pricing, product features, commission for salesmen, advertising and any other lever we could pull to generate a sale. However, given the very long-term nature of the liabilities of life assurance products we had a department of actuaries who managed the risks and consequences of product design and promotion. The balance between the two areas was maintained despite much healthy conflict. The nature of the relationship between sales and actuaries was such that both were required to have power. This ensured that products were competitive, profitable and no time bombs were being created. A marketing executive will tell you that some of the most powerful words in advertising are free, chocolate, new and sex. Another powerful word is 'guaranteed'. Such a word can stir and/or reassure customers depending on its intention. It can have a wonderfully uplifting impact on sales. Unfortunately, the word also has a very dark side. By using it you change the basic economics of a business and create the time bomb that can cause a major crisis, as at Equitable Life. So, hypothetically, if the promise was made by Equitable Life in order to boost sales, why did nobody manage the consequences of issuing the guarantee? Perhaps the incentive schemes in place rewarded the sales generated and the profit booked but not the potential consequences if the assumptions about how much the guarantees might cost proved to be incorrect? As we have already discussed a number of times, assumptions about the future should be treated with the same degree of care and respect as radioactive waste.

Before moving on we can consider two more instances where the basic economic fundamentals and related incentives create a crisis. One has happened; many would argue the other is happening. The sub-prime credit crisis and collapse of Lehman Brothers was based on the assumptions that securitization removed risk from the financial system and poor credit quality could be covered by rising house prices. In addition, the profits being made by the whole industry from securitization were huge and paid out immediately, not when the full economics of the deals eventually played out. Basic economics were wrongly coupled with incentives that made everybody ignore the risks.

The second crisis relates to the global environment and related usage of finite resources such as oil, gas, land and fresh water. When the accounting system still used to this day was first described by the Italian friar, Luca Pacioli, in 1494, it did not include the consequential impact of a company's activities on the resources it did not have to pay for. Even today there is no role in the financial statements of corporations for the carbon producing impacts of their operations or the replacement cost element of the fossil fuels that they are using. Since the Industrial Revolution altered the scale and consequential impact of humankind's activities on the environment, companies have been able to produce 'profits' without counting the total cost of their actions. The assumption has been that the consequences of the actions would not lead to any form of crisis. Sounds a little bit like what might have happened at Equitable Life.

Before moving on to the next internal driver of a potential crisis, what can we learn that is of practical use in avoiding a crisis due to either of the first two?

Corporate breakdowns cannot be entirely predicted or avoided but there may be some common traits that increase the potential for a breakdown. The first of these is a failure to take a detailed enough 360 degree view of the business. This results in leaders making decisions about things they do not actually understand well enough. This prompts some thoughts. Perhaps some decisions should be made by the people who actually know the business rather than those that think they know the business. An intention to stay close to the roots of the business is not worth anything unless you take meaningful action to do something about this. If you believe the mantra that what gets measured gets managed then perhaps you should shine a light on how managers spend their time. Taking a fully rounded view of a business requires a leader to take multiple viewpoints. Any one manager is highly unlikely to be fully qualified in interpreting the signals that are coming from each viewpoint. This means that we all, especially if we are the CEO, have to be open to continual learning and not consider that we know, or are expected to know, all the answers.

In Chapter 6 we will discuss the $100 model of a business. This tool is intended to help you think about the basic underlying economics of a market or company. The intention is to use common business sense to identify opportunities and risks. If for a long time a company seems to be able to make returns above the market norms, what time bombs might it be storing up? Witness Enron, Worldcom, Madoff, etc. If you perceive a potentially unbalanced economic situation then you should be on the lookout for an incentive system that is encouraging people to maintain but not question the status quo until the bomb blows up. It takes real courage and awareness to do this within your own company.

Management optimism

The third internal driver of a crisis is the predisposition of many managers to make over-optimistic assumptions about the future and a common trait in relation to identifying potential corporate breakdown.

As I said earlier, a business only makes a profit if it takes some risk. Anything that is certain does not usually hold out much opportunity. Because of that it is healthy and valuable for leaders and managers to take a positive view of the future and how their product or service will grow and create wealth.

In his book, *The Fortune at the Bottom of the Pyramid* (2004), the leading academic C K Prahalad discusses a Brazilian retail company called Casas Bahia. The overwhelming majority of sales at this business are to customers to whom most other businesses would not extend credit. Casas Bahia takes the view that the poorest people in the country have a right to the everyday household items that many people take for granted: televisions, furniture, homewares and the like. The company also takes the positive view that its customers will pay back the credit extended to them. This optimistic view of the world has allowed the company to grow financially and make a valuable contribution to the poorest families in Brazil. This type of optimism is to be welcomed and encouraged.

The kind of optimism that leads to a potential crisis is not the same kind that Casas Bahia has displayed. Unhealthy optimism is found in leadership teams that make assumptions about future sales, margins, costs and cash flows that push middle managers to make poor resource judgements. When a sales director is convinced under duress by the rest of the board that his revenue forecasts show a lack of ambition, the resulting reforecast could well be viewed within the boardroom as merely a healthy challenge to the business. In a very short period of time this healthy challenge can become the base case projection. This will be put into the budget process and emerge in individual objectives and incentive plans. The supply chain planners will convert the forecasts into stock holding units and volumes and spend capital on the new transport, warehouse facilities and IT systems required. The marketing department will calculate the market share, consumer awareness recall statistics and resultant advertising spend that will be required to drive the sales required. The sales numbers might even start to leak outside to investors via road shows and presentations. Thus the healthy challenge from the board has resulted in resources, people, cash and opportunities, being spent to support a given level of sales. The leadership and corporate commitment to this level of sales is now absolute. As actual data and results start to indicate that sales might not reach the levels forecast, usually no one wants to listen. The company prefers to believe that such short-term underperformance will be corrected next week, next month or as a result of all the additional actions that are being taken. Such additional actions add more cost, resource and managerial commitment to the sales number. Often, the only thing that will break the spell and allow action to be taken to size the resources to actual sales levels is either a change of management or a crisis.

A word of warning. A leader who is displaying unhealthy optimism will often not recognize it, confusing the need for a positive mental attitude with unhealthy optimism and, when the issue is raised, will shoot the messenger.

Lack of sensitivity

This driver of a crisis is where leaders and managers think they are sensitive to changes in the market but actually miss critical trends and changes. Such a lack of corporate sensitivity can manifest itself in being slow to understand changing customer needs, expanding too slowly or too fast into new countries and markets, in losing staff as ways of working change or in being unable to set the right cost base. Being sensitive means continually scanning the market and your own business to pick up emerging trends and issues. It is also the ability to make sense of disparate sets of conflicting data and take some action as a result. In Chapter 9 we will explore a model to help you deliver improved results by identifying new possibilities for your business. The foundation for this model is the relationships that you build inside and outside of your organization. The companies that are not only highly sensitive to changes in the market but also considered in their response tend to be better at avoiding a crisis and profiting from uncertain times. Witness the amazing success of Goldman Sachs during the credit crunch.

Some organizations have a very action-orientated culture. This is an important characteristic because results only flow from actions being taken. However, sometimes such cultures focus too much on taking action and not enough on scanning and interpreting market trends and changes. Over time this can result in falling market share, shrinking margins and having the wrong assets in the wrong places, all of which will lead to cash issues and a crisis.

The classic examples of lack of corporate foresight can be interesting thought stimulation models for you and your leadership team. IBM lost out to Microsoft in the PC market. Microsoft lost out to Google in the internet search market. Who might Google lose out to? What information would you seek out to help you gain the earliest insights into a threat to Google's dominance? Regulatory issues like Microsoft has faced? A total alternative to Google's search based advertising model, just ask Yellow Pages how they feel? A model that shares revenue with the person browsing? A free netbook if you use an alternative search engine to Google, maybe sponsored by a mobile broadband operator? What is more important to a user – using the Google search engine or receiving a free computer or free mobile broadband access? Be as innovative as you can with your team about trying to identify places to scan to see if Google could be toppled. Once the creative juices are flowing you can then apply the same process to your own company and market position. Not who the competitor might be and how they could destroy your market position. Rather, where would you go to find the earliest signs of a challenge to your market position?

Chapter 6 specifically focuses on how to scan the environment and become more sensitive to the factors that could impact your business.

5 Where to start after a crisis – making the right promises

The two principal objectives of this book are to help you, as a leader, avoid a crisis and to recover effectively after one. At this point we move from a focus on identifying potential crises and avoiding them to what to do after a crisis has occurred. In this chapter we will look at a framework to use in planning your recovery and thinking about the promises you can make to stakeholders after a crisis. Deciding what promises to make is the first of the five areas of leadership expertise we will consider:

- making the right promises;
- gathering multiple, new viewpoints;

- core business skills;
- delivering results through relationships;
- rebuilding trust with authentic communication.

Each of these areas is an opportunity to improve your own effectiveness and improve the skills and capabilities of your team and organization. This chapter splits broadly into two halves – where to start your recovery plan and making the right promises.

Where to start – earning the right

My experience is that even in times of extreme uncertainty it is worth the time to make some sort of plan, rather than just focusing on fighting the fires. If you are to progress from solely responding to the events that are happening, you will have to plan, if only to buy yourself some more time. In his book *The Leadership Moment* (1999), Michael Useem describes how, in 1949, the American fire fighter Wagner Dodge saved the lives of some of his colleagues trapped by a forest fire. The circumstances are well reported upon elsewhere. In summary, a series of decisions and events resulted in Dodge and his crew facing extreme danger from a wild fire. Dodge used an 'escape fire' to protect himself and some others from the main fire. An escape fire is one that is used to clear a protective area of land and any materials that the main fire would otherwise burn through. Effectively, the main fire jumps over the protective area produced by the ring of grassland already burnt by the escape fire. Even in a moment of extreme danger, Dodge thought through a plan to protect both himself and others rather than just focusing on fighting the main fire.

Even when you are facing the heat of your business crisis and the telephones are ringing off their hooks, you will need to find some time to make an initial plan. The plan should focus on buying you more time. At the most extreme, on day one you will have to build and communicate a plan that gives you a few extra days. In those few days you need to have a plan that will convince the people who need convincing to give you a week. In a week you can build a plan that should buy you a month. With a month you can not only start to shape a possible view of a better and stronger future but also start to deliver some positive momentum.

The business risk is when the plan you build is not appropriate for the situation you face. When faced with a wild fire about to engulf you, your plan should be focused on the next few minutes. Some management teams find it difficult to make this rapid adjustment to their historic planning methods and styles. When I advised a European telecoms business just after the tech bubble burst in 2001, the company and its corporate finance advisors were focused on preparing a plan based on a valuation using a five year financial projection. The objective was to convince the existing shareholders to put in over $400 million of new money. This was a critical part of the recovery plan – but not the first thing to be doing. Enough time and cash had to be generated to give the shareholders sufficient time to consider the valuation and five year plan properly. Trade creditors and the bank were worried about being paid next week and whether the monthly payroll could be financed. Before earning the right to talk about the sales projections for five years the company had to convince the most pressing and relevant stakeholders to support them for the next three weeks. In those three weeks we could provide a route map for the next six months. In the six months we had time to convince the various stakeholders about value in the medium and longer term.

This is the key point about where to start in planning after a crisis. You have to earn the right from stakeholders to move on to the next step. Trying to run before you can walk can make the crisis worse as stakeholders wonder whether you, as a management team, understand the priorities and order of issues that you are facing. Put another way, stakeholders may feel you are not competent to lead the recovery. To earn the confidence of stakeholders you have to address the concerns at the front of their minds, even if you do not think they are the concerns they should have. Remember the definition of a crisis we have been using. The turning point is when stakeholders' key assumptions about your business change. After assumptions change, stakeholders will be in a vacuum as to what ones they should be making. Your job is to earn back the right to be trusted to provide reliable input into their thinking.

How to get it wrong

In 2009 the UK parliament suffered a severe crisis of public confidence over members', MPs, expenses. The public had for many years assumed that MPs were generally honest about the expenses they claimed or, at the very least, there was a system of controls that ensured that the expenses were genuine. When details of the MPs' claims were leaked there was a rapid turning point where the public changed its assumptions. In the crisis of confidence that followed, the leaders within parliament needed to show they had a plan to restore the confidence of the public in its representatives. To do this properly, in a considered manner, would require some months to achieve. Parliament would have to earn the right to this extra time as a start to regaining public confidence. The short term plan to do this was, unfortunately, at best ill-conceived and at worst completely non-existent. The way the information about expenses was officially released actually served to further destroy public trust as the data was so heavily edited that, in the absence of the full leaked information, most of the scandals and wrongdoings would not have been uncovered. While the public was seeking assurance of a fresh approach they were served up further evidence of a system that was happy to treat the electorate as people to be kept in the dark. The plan, such as it was, did not focus on earning the right to build trust and gain more time from the media and public.

First steps

In a business context we can set out a 10 point list to follow in building the initial phase recovery plan:

1. How much time and cash do I have?
2. Who are the most relevant stakeholders and why?
3. What are those stakeholders seeking in the short term?
4. What can I deliver in the short term?
5. What needs to be done to earn the right to the next phase?
6. What should I promise to stakeholders at this point?
7. How will I communicate best to those stakeholders?
8. How do I ensure delivery of what I now choose to promise?
9. Deliver and communicate.
10. Go back to the beginning and build the next phase of the plan.

Each iteration of the plan will use the same steps but with an adjustment to the timeframe depending on how much extra or less time and cash you then have.

This series of steps is based on experience of helping companies manage through and after a crisis but, more importantly, from discussions with some of the people who are critical stakeholders for you after a crisis. I have interviewed a range of bankers, investors, creditors, advisors, directors and communications specialists about what they want from leaders of business after a crisis. One of my favourite interviews was with the head of work-out banking for a leading international commercial institution. He takes over a situation for the bank when a company has defaulted on its promises to the bank; covenant breaches, excess drawing on facilities or non-payment of interest or principal.

There are two things he wants to see from management straight after a crisis has hit. First, a flow of information that is available to help him provide more time for the bank to help the company. A vacuum of data or wrongly focused information accentuates the sense that management is not in control and forces decisions to be taken earlier than necessary. Second, a realization from management that it will have to lead and behave in a different and appropriate manner. Basically, has management woken up and smelled the coffee? The assumptions that the bank made about the business have changed. Has management also made the mental readjustment to its new circumstances? Remember how the leaders of the major US automakers when first called to Washington to discuss a bailout in 2009 arrived in their corporate private jets. Such behaviour would not demonstrate that those leaders understood the situation they found themselves in after a crisis.

In their book *Why Should Anybody be Led by You?* (2006), Rob Goffee and Gareth Jones explain how the behaviour of leaders is minutely studied by all the people around them. The negative side of this is that if your behaviour does not match the situation or what is expected, many people will notice. The upside is that small changes in your behaviour can have a very positive impact. It is these changes in leadership behaviour that we will examine in this and the following chapters as part of our discussion about the five areas of leadership expertise that could help you manage successfully after a crisis:

1. *Making the right promises.* In the current situation do we understand what all our key stakeholders are focusing on and the promises they are seeking from us and our company?
2. *Gathering multiple, new viewpoints.* As leaders, have we taken a complete 360 degree view of the business, its stakeholders and the market in the current environment? A failure to consider all perspectives may restrict the range of ideas and solutions that are available.

3. *Core business skills.* Do we have the necessary expertise, experience and insights to make decisions about the issues that matter most in today's environment?
4. *Delivering results through relationships.* What are the right implementation models and leadership styles to employ to ensure that the promises we make are delivered?
5. *Rebuilding trust through authentic communication.* How will we build and maintain the level of trust with employees, customers, suppliers, lenders and investors that will be necessary to deliver results in uncertain times?

At the very start of the recovery phase after a crisis your leadership will be under intense scrutiny. Questions will be asked about whether you and the existing management team are the right people to lead the business in these circumstances. These five areas are intended to help you be the leader that your company needs to build and deliver the recovery plan.

In this chapter we will examine the first of these five areas of leadership expertise: making the right promises. The truth is you will not have all the information you need at the start of the recovery phase to make all the right promises. However, you need to be thinking from the beginning how you will select and balance the promises that you do eventually make.

Making the right promises

In the normal course of business, a leader is constantly making and trying to deliver on a set of promises to key stakeholders. The challenge is to try to give a reasonable return to all stakeholders. The choices of what promises to make and, critically, the delivery against those promises is the fundamental core of what a business does. In many ways, you could say that the principal role of a leader is to make, balance and deliver business promises. Such promises could include:

- What can I promise to investors and lenders to attract and retain the right financing?
- What will customers expect and require from our company in order to buy from us?
- How can I attract, motivate and retain the right people?
- What will suppliers want from me and what can I promise them?

The tool we shall use in this leadership expertise area considers the interactions between four categories of stakeholder: customers, investors and lenders, employees and suppliers. The manager and leader sits in the middle of each group's expectations and tries to balance the promises made and delivered to each of them. At any one point the situation is probably unbalanced in favour of one of the stakeholder groups. The balance of return to the stakeholders will constantly shift as the company introduces new products, changes prices, alters employee benefits and supplier contracts and announces its dividend for investors. The normal ebb and flow of business will cause the balance of promises and return to be constantly shifting.

However, the promises need to balance out over the medium-term, otherwise the business is likely to face a crisis. I gave an example earlier. Every customer would like to receive a top quality product for no charge, forever. But how would a company providing such a deal be able to pay dividends, interest, salaries or its suppliers? A leader is always adjusting the balance of promises and seeking new ways and ideas that can increase the overall value to all of the stakeholders and maintain a medium-term balanced position.

In Chapter 1 I suggested an analogy for this skill was like learning to use a 'balance board' or 'wobble board' at the gym. I make no apologies for reintroducing it here together with the graphic representation in Figure 5.1.

```
                    Customers
                       and
                    Consumers
                        ▲
                        │
  Investors             │
     and    ◄──── Business Leader ────► Suppliers
   Lenders             │
                        │
                        ▼
                    Employees
```

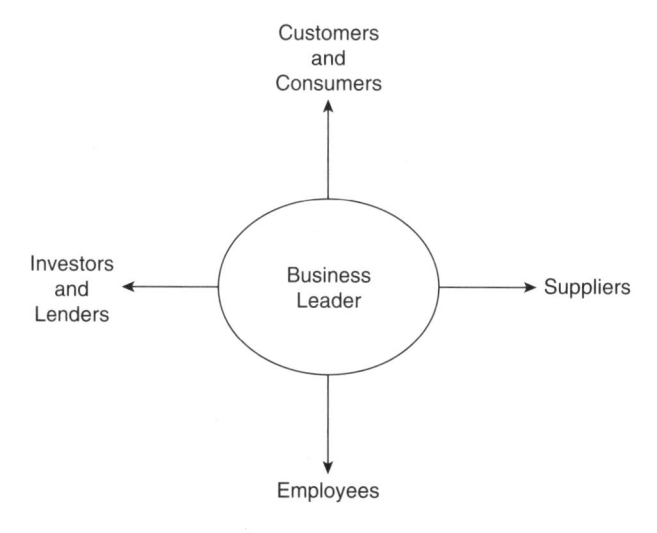

Figure 5.1 Leadership wobble board

As you progress through your management career you will develop skills and experience which will enable you to control ever more difficult leadership wobble boards. In New York a few years ago I listened to a talk by the then CEO of Wal-Mart, Lee Scott. The majority of the speech was about managing the more than 2 million employees that the business had and the significant political, social and union pressures that were placed upon it as a result. This CEO's wobble board was equivalent to running a country. The skill of the Wal-Mart leadership team to manage 175 million customers worldwide, a 10-year record of dividend growth, the 2 million employees and thousands and thousands of suppliers has to be of Olympic standard wobble board control. Even in the normal course of business selecting, balancing and delivering upon promises to such a diverse and large group of stakeholders is a significant challenge.

I also said the extra challenge for a leader after a crisis is that somebody has just kicked the wobble board, very hard, and may continue to do so. A crisis will destabilize the positions of the different stakeholders and restrict your ability to deliver on the promises previously made. To help with the start of your planning after a crisis we can spend a little time thinking about each of the key stakeholders, how they might feel and the promises you might consider making to them.

Customers

Customers are the only sustainable source of value for all the other stakeholders that you have to make promises to. Employees and suppliers are paid from the profits of transacting with your customers. Customers eventually pay for your bank interest and dividends. Therefore, the question of what promises to make to customers after a crisis in order to maintain sales, is central to the success of your recovery plan. For a promise to customers to make business sense it needs to:

- provide value to the customers, so they will stay with you or return if they have left;
- be capable of being delivered by you at a profit;
- generate sufficient cash to pay all the other stakeholders their promised return.

The types of promises that you make to customers will have many parameters including quality, price, service and brand reputation. On a simplified basis the model I have used with companies and executives is to consider the promises made against four of these parameters – quality, value, service and innovation (QVSI).

We can use the example of children's confectionery to illustrate the QVSI model. If you have young children, then any visit to the grocery store could well end up with a discussion about the selection of a sweet as a reward for their good behaviour. The myriad of choices facing both the young child and you is bewildering. For my children, however, there was always a constant favourite – a Kinder Surprise chocolate egg. These are sold across the world, except in the United States. For those of you that have not come across this particular confectionery delight, it is a small hollow chocolate egg with a plastic container inside. The container holds the surprise, which has historically been a small plastic toy. From the child's perspective why would they choose this egg over a different sweet or chocolate? On a QVSI basis it might be:

- Quality. The chocolate tastes sweet and acceptable, a guaranteed small sugar rush.
- Value. Not only is there chocolate but also a surprise toy. This is a purchase that has added attractions.
- Service. The toys are normally part of a collectable series, with a piece of paper inside the egg showing all the possible toys to collect in that series. I can aim to acquire the full set, fuelling increased follow-on purchases.
- Innovation. Not only do the toys require construction but since the development of the internet there is a secret code inside each egg which allows me to play exclusive games on the Kinder Surprise website.

All-in-all, a very compelling purchase for a young child. However, the economic buyer is normally the parent rather than the child. What does the QVSI analysis say from a parent's perspective?

- Quality. The egg consists of only a small amount of milk chocolate so it will not fill up my child before lunch. It looks quite natural and is not a poisonous looking colour like some of the other sweets on offer.
- Value. The egg is about 50 per cent more expensive than a simple chocolate bar but it is still only about a dollar.
- Service. This purchase will entertain and engage my child for possibly hours after the purchase, as they add the new toy to their collection.

- Innovation. The games on the internet seem almost educational and far better than some of the other stuff that is out there.

To me, who has purchased hundreds of these eggs for my four children, the promises that Kinder makes are both compelling and delivered on. The QVSI model provides a tool for you to deconstruct the promises or attributes of your offering to customers. This can then be compared to competitors' offerings and customer needs and preferences in a post-crisis world. To achieve this we use the QVSI model as a starting point. Customers may ask themselves after the crisis:

- Quality. Will this company's products still do what they have always promised to do? Is it a risk now for me to continue to purchase from this business?
- Value. Will the company continue to trade or support this product? If not, then this could turn out to be a very expensive purchase.
- Service. Will after-sales support and guarantees be honoured?
- Innovation. This is a long-term purchasing decision for me; will the upgrades and product development support be available in the future?

All of these types of questions, and many more, will be in the minds of your consumers – private, corporate and government. As you start out on the rebuilding of your business after a crisis you will need to think about what promises need to be made again to customers and what new ones might be needed to retain their loyalty.

Investors and lenders

The second stakeholder group to consider is investors and lenders. This group provides finance in the shape of equity, bonds, bank facilities and letters of credit that allow a business to operate. The type of promises that companies make to investors and lenders tend to be financial in nature, for example, dividend expectations, loan interest payments, covenant compliance and expected share value creation. However, investors and lenders are increasingly interested in the brand and supply chain integrity of the companies they invest in.

We shall return to the reaction of financial stakeholders to a crisis a number of times in this book. The reason for this is that they are often the most important short-term stakeholders in ensuring stability after a crisis and allowing the time to build a foundation for a recovery.

As you start out on your recovery plan preparation the first important thing to do is understand what the lenders can do to help you in your turnaround and what they can do to remove control from your hands. We will discuss this in relation to core business skills in Chapters 7 and 8.

Employees

The third stakeholder group is the staff of the company. The promises to employees can include a salary or wage, a safe and equitable place to work, development opportunities and consultation. After a crisis, your people will be the ones to design and deliver a recovery plan and you may have to make and keep promises to them that were not necessary in less turbulent times.

As with investors and lenders, we will speak throughout the book about your people including the senior team, middle managers and front line staff. Most importantly in Chapter 9 we will look at how to deliver better business results through improved relationships with your employees. Chapter 10 considers the ways to rebuild trust with all stakeholders after a crisis.

Suppliers

The fourth stakeholder group is suppliers. It includes trade suppliers and their credit insurers as well as organizations that supply your company with a 'licence' to operate, such as regulators and governments, which we discussed in Chapter 3. As with the other three categories of stakeholder, understanding the current position of your suppliers, their potential reactions and the impact of their actions on your recovery planning are necessary first steps to take.

Starting at the beginning

The selecting and making of new promises after a crisis will test your common business sense. This 'gut feel' about what is the right thing to do is a crucial ingredient in leadership and decision making. However, gut feel is also a dangerous way to make decisions if you do not have all of the facts to hand. The next chapter looks at how you can develop a 360 degree view of your business and market after a crisis.

6 Gathering multiple new viewpoints

The second area of leadership expertise is about expanding the insights and knowledge you have about the crisis and the potential recovery options. This should enable you to make better choices and plans. I reiterate, the two resources in scarce supply after a crisis are cash and time. In order to increase the supply of both you will have to take actions, communicate effectively and deliver some early results. Action is not, however, a complete substitute for thought and insight. The actions you take have to be smarter than the ones that took the business into a crisis. If the actions involve the same people with the same knowledge and the same outlook on the business as before the crisis, why will the results be any better? A crisis provides you with the right and the opportunity to take fresh perspectives and approaches. What a shame if you miss that opportunity because you spend all of your time acting as a fire fighter.

I am not suggesting that you spend the first six months after the crisis on a voyage of indulgent research. I am saying that unless you find fresh insights your plan is at a higher risk of failure. As with all matters of business, and in particular after a crisis when you are under greater levels of scrutiny, everything is a question of balance and perception. You need to ensure that stakeholders who expect rapid action feel that you are taking the necessary urgent measures. As a leader you must ensure that people in your team are, for example, totally in control of cash forecasting and management. As importantly, you need to make sure that stakeholders 'perceive' that you are in total control of cash.

In addition, as a leader you need to make sure there is time available to seek out the fresh insights that you and the team will need. Given that time is always short in a crisis, you need to make the best use of the resources you apply to gaining new perspectives. The framework set out in this chapter is one way of trying to use that scarce time to best effect. There are a couple of important principles about any approach that you use to gain fresh insights. First, make sure that you take a 360 degree viewpoint, which will require going to a wide variety of perspectives. Second, seek out new and different people, data and opinions. Sometimes it is the things on the periphery that are the most relevant but also the most difficult to find and interpret.

On this point it is worth considering some of the ways that military and secret intelligence is gathered. When a problem is encountered that requires intelligence to solve it, the classical business consulting methodology will be to brief a team of internal and external managers to define the problem, gather data, analyse it as a team and propose a hypothesis or solution. This has the long held advantage of many minds being better than one. The drawback is that you may end up missing out on some of the more extreme viewpoints. In addition, the conclusions and recommendations might have been corrupted by 'group thinking'. Group thinking can result in a consensus style solution which keeps most people happy but actually obscures the more radical solutions that have a better chance of success.

A secret intelligence services process for gathering insights can take a different approach. A brief is prepared defining the intelligence being sought. That brief is then given to a number of separate agents to investigate. No agent is aware of the identity of the others and they do not come together as a team to produce a consolidated viewpoint. Instead, they all prepare separate reports based on their own discussions and findings. This produces a much wider set of viewpoints and possible overlapping insights that the people issuing the brief can consider and put together with other more traditional forms of intelligence they have. In a business context this would be like the CEO commissioning 10 different individuals with the same brief to go out and interview, research and prepare their own views on an issue. In fact, there is at least one consultancy firm that operates in this way for corporate clients all around the world. I am not proposing that this would work as a methodology for you or your company. I am suggesting that you consider carefully the different methodologies available to collect fresh insights before you choose which one to use.

The approach discussed in this chapter is inspired by the game of Trivial Pursuit™. In the game you need to be able to answer questions on a wide variety of subjects in order to win. Being a specialist in sports and nothing else is unlikely to win you the game. In business, being only a supply chain specialist or wizard accountant is unlikely to give you all of the perspectives that you will need to build and deliver a successful recovery plan.

The proposition is that in order to make the best leadership decisions after a crisis you need to consider the factors facing your business from multiple viewpoints. In addition, you need to be able to understand how those multiple views interact with each other. As said earlier, if you come from a marketing background then it is most natural to see the business issues and potential solutions to a crisis through the filter of a marketing professional. Accountants might see the problems and challenges through a financial viewpoint. If you can hold multiple viewpoints of the business and market, and help your teams to do the same, you open up the possibility of generating more innovative and deliverable actions. If you accept the need to take a 360 degree view of your business, the question then arises: what are the different viewpoints you need to consider?

You will recall from Chapter 1 that as in the game of Trivial Pursuit™ six viewpoints are examined here and you and your team need to test yourselves to see that you have sufficient knowledge to answer the questions that arise from each viewpoint (see Figure 6.1).

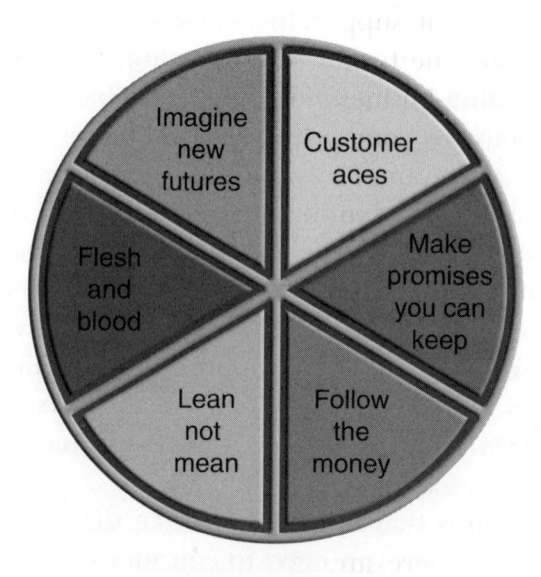

Figure 6.1 Six viewpoints model

Let me remind you what the six viewpoints in the tool are:

- *Customer aces.* How will consumers and enterprises behave during and after the crisis?
- *Make promises you can keep.* How are plans and decisions made and do we deliver on our promises as a business?
- *Follow the money.* Where and how is cash generated and used within our business?
- *Lean not mean.* How is our cost base structured and what could be done to change it?
- *Flesh and blood.* How will the people outside and inside our business be affected by the crisis and how might they react?
- *Imagine new futures.* As we look towards the future, what is the transformational change that our company could make following the crisis?

It is important to consider the whole of your business from each particular viewpoint. For example, when considering the customer aces viewpoint it is not sufficient just to look at products, pricing and service. Customers will also have a view on management, supply chain, cost structures, your values and finances and the future. You must consider a customer's total view of your business and the market to start to gain valuable insights for your recovery plan. There may be additional, or more relevant, viewpoints for you and your teams to understand in respect of your particular industry or geography. For example, the attitude of governments and regulators may be a critical viewpoint for you to assess. The important elements of this tool are that you as a leader take the time to articulate the viewpoints that need to be assessed, keeping it to no more than six or seven, and can explain the nature of each viewpoint to your team. We shall now examine each of these viewpoints and consider the tools you can use in each.

Before we start, there are two things to remember. I have already emphasized you need to leave the boardroom and expend some shoe leather in order to gain valuable insights. You will need to speak to people at all levels within the business and outside the company. You also need to approach your research with an open mind and be prepared to listen actively. It is a waste of your time, and likely to be detrimental to morale, if you say you have come to hear people's opinions and then spend the time telling them what you think. As you go around try to leave every interaction having learned as much as you can and having made the person feel more valued in the way that you have listened to them.

Customer aces

The first viewpoint that you can take is the obvious one – what is the customer's perspective on your business? A great deal of research will tell you that while most senior management teams consider that they and their business are customer focused, when customers are asked they do not think many of the businesses serving them actually do focus on the customer. When talking in earlier chapters about what a crisis is and what causes it, I described the tipping point as when customers change a key assumption they have made about a company, a product or a service. The consequence of such a change in belief by customers is likely to be them ceasing to buy or demanding a change in the terms on which they will do business. Such changes could result in such a loss of business or profitability that a financial crisis comes about. The publicity resulting from a change in customer assumptions may also create a public relations disaster. Our first action, therefore, is to gather a list of all the assumptions that a customer is making about your company, products, services, pricing, terms, competitors and markets.

In order to perform some mental warm-ups for this part of the research we can start with some of the best known changes in customer assumptions that created crises for the companies involved. One of the tipping points has been the move from buying things that are 'good' to 'good enough'. By this I mean a change from consumers' requirements for a product or service to satisfy more than just their essential needs; 'a good product' to focusing focus on the absolute essentials, 'a good enough product'.

In the US automotive sector, for decades the low price of fuel meant that consumers could indulge their desire for large vehicles without being too worried about the running costs. This segment of large pick-ups and sports utility vehicles earned super profits for the manufacturers. As you may remember, in Chapter 3 we looked at super profit earning as one of the early warning signs of a crisis. The rapid rise in the price of oil resulted in a tipping point in consumer behaviour. Whilst many would still prefer a large car with a huge engine, it was good enough for their transport needs to buy a smaller, more economical car. This shift in spending to a segment where the major US manufacturers were less competitive and the profit margins smaller, was one of the factors contributing to the crisis they all eventually faced. In short-haul airline flights the same shift from good to good enough has happened. Many consumers are happy to trade assigned seating, meals and lounges for a lower ticket price. When I clothe my children for school, it is now possible to buy trousers, shoes, shirts and a jumper for less than $20 in total from a hypermarket. The quality is very average but it is good enough for what is needed. Many companies serving the consumer with products or services that provided a good level of benefit have suffered as competitors have produced cheaper alternatives that are good enough. In such circumstances the companies facing falling sales had made the assumption that consumers would continue to pay for the additional benefits they were providing, rather than take the cheaper price.

The task is to collect all of the relevant assumptions that customers are making and then seek out evidence of how such assumptions might change or how your company might be able to change customer assumptions to its advantage. The table below is a generic list of the areas that you could look at when taking the customers' viewpoint of your business and the assumptions that they make. Clearly, you will need to adapt the table for your own circumstances. In fact, compiling the table and adapting it as you learn more is a valuable part of the process. A table is set out below and the assumptions have been filled in to provide an example for a four star airport hotel which is part of one of the well known international chains. The customer is a family looking for an overnight stay before flying off on holiday. Note that the second column is not the management's objective for what customers should think but rather your insight into what customers actually think, based on some research (see Table 6.1).

To add to this example based on actual data from a larger assignment I worked on, the historic split of bookings from families staying one night and parking for the period of their holiday was over 20 per cent of the hotel's total income. This percentage was at good prices and contributed proportionally higher to overall net margins. Over a period of 12 months, the bookings in this area had collapsed and the overall impact was to make the hotel only marginally profitable. In such circumstance where would you go to seek out views and insights about how to rectify this problem? In doing so two things should become clear. Did customers actually hold the views that management believed they did? Were customers making any other assumptions that were important to them and which management did not understand or value?

The most obvious way to understand the situation was to actually check-in and stay with your family or ask a friend, but

Table 6.1 Taking the customer's viewpoint

Customer Viewpoint	Your Insight about the Customer's View
Brand:	They feel more comfortable with a well known brand and are prepared to pay a small premium for it
Price:	The convenience of an airport location is worth paying something extra for
Deal:	Packages with parking are good value for money
Functionality:	The family rooms mean I do not have to book more than one room to accommodate everybody
Direct alternatives:	There are only two hotels located at the airport terminal
Do without:	Get up very early and drive to my flight without an overnight stay
Good enough:	There is a budget hotel located three miles from the airport
Service:	The brand promises a high level of service and I will be stressed travelling with my family, so staff should understand this
Delivery:	It is easy to check-in, check-out, my children will be fed and sleep well, without too much stress, and I will catch my plane
After-sales service:	My car will be secure and convenient in the car park while I am away
What my friends will think:	Smart parent who started their holiday well and did not waste their money

not a colleague, to do the same with their family. To cut directly to what had happened, management learned by experiencing the service themselves that the customer also made one extra assumption. While the hotel saw the one night stay as a convenient way for families to be ready for the flight the following day, the family, especially the children, viewed this stay as the beginning of the holiday that they had been excited about for months. This assumption meant they hoped the hotel would treat them, or the children at least, as being on holiday, not just as guests on a convenient one night stay. The hotel was geared towards the 80 per cent of revenue that came from business travellers and the overall customer service was focused on their requirements. The hotel could not afford playrooms, nanny services, or clowns to entertain the children. Where could the management go to find inspiration to make the experience better for families and increase the profitability of the one night stays?

Two places stood out – Disney Hotels and McDonald's. Without incurring vast new capital expenditure, they learned some easy things to do to improve service and profitability, including steps at check-in desks so small children could see what was going on; cheap but highly prized packs of crayons, colouring book and activities; in-room dining packages that included quick and child-friendly food in a colourful box and a kid's movie from the in-room entertainment system. This last idea also encouraged parents to order a meal from the room service menu, increasing overall spend – thank you McDonald's. Most importantly, the hotels explained to staff what this particular customer group wanted. Two things happened. Average spend per family increased and the parents had been given great stories to tell to their friends about how the hotel really made a difference to the start of their holiday – right down to the child-friendly chocolate on the pillow. The extra capital cost to the hotel was almost nil but the additional revenue was highly profitable. It also created a sense of fun that the staff enjoyed. How was this achieved? Not from the boardroom but through understanding all of the important assumptions that the customer was really making and taking inexpensive action to make those assumptions a reality.

So how do you go about understanding the customer viewpoint? There are dozens of consulting tools available for you to use.

The trick is to pick the right ones and use them with the right frame of mind. Go and visit and talk to lots of different people around the business. Spend time actually being a customer. List out all the assumptions customers are making about your product or service. Most importantly, do not forget that we all like to have a story to tell our friends or colleagues about a buying experience. Unfortunately, these are often negative stories about service, quality or value for money. If you, as a company, do not seek to create the stories that you want a customer to re-tell dozens of times about your service or product then you are leaving what the customer will say entirely up to chance. What do you want customers to say to their friends and colleagues? What do your managers think customers are saying? What are they actually saying? Not the worst place to start when considering your customers after your business has hit a crisis.

Making promises you can keep

The second viewpoint you can take to gather fresh insights on the business and to build a recovery plan is how the business makes decisions and promises to stakeholders and whether it has a track record of delivery. If you are facing a crisis situation then something has already gone wrong in the making and delivery of promises.

There are two areas you can review to help understand things from this viewpoint: the budget process and the forecast process. Before looking into each of these it is worth examining the thinking behind this viewpoint. The analogy we have been using to describe the role of a business leader is balancing on a wobble board of competing promises between stakeholders, investors and lenders, customers, employees and suppliers. Remember Figure 6.2?

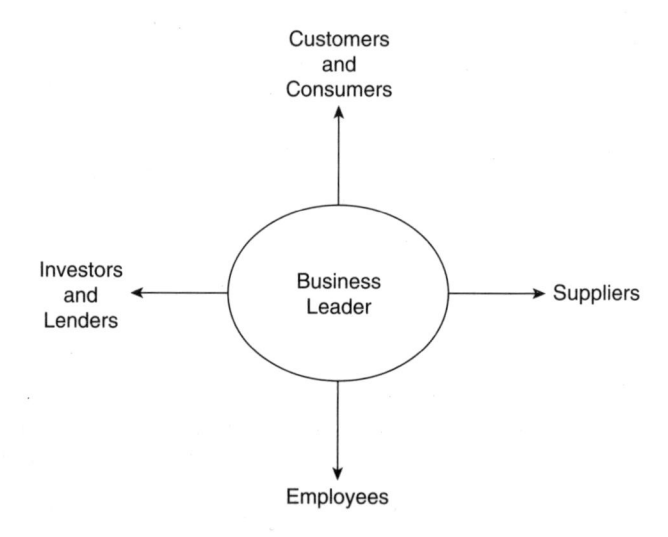

```
                    Customers
                       and
                    Consumers
                        ↑
                        |
Investors                                    
  and    ←——  Business Leader  ——→  Suppliers
Lenders                                      
                        |
                        ↓
                    Employees
```

Figure 6.2 Leadership wobble board

You will remember the point that the leadership and management wobble board is always unbalanced at any given time and the leader's job is to readjust to ensure that over the medium term all the stakeholders receive a fair return from the business. I also said that after a crisis it will feel as though somebody has kicked the board and the five areas of leadership expertise described in this book are intended as a guide to help you restore some form of balance. As you build a recovery plan it should be insightful to study how your company makes choices and promises, communicates those promises and monitors delivery. Such processes, whether formal, informal or ad hoc, are an essential part of the culture of any business. Making changes to what promises are made and how they are formulated, communicated and monitored will cause changes to the fabric of the company. This may be a necessary and important part of the recovery plan. However, making changes without an insight into what the impacts will be could have a further destabilizing impact.

The other thing to bear in mind as you look at things from this viewpoint is the use of language. I have very deliberately used the term 'promise' as it should carry a more emotional resonance with people than objective, budget or forecast. The making and delivery of business promises goes to the very heart and soul of a business and after any crisis should be something that interests a business leader greatly.

The budget process

Despite decades of management research, ideas and executive education the most powerful and all-pervasive management tool remains the annual budget process. In most established companies this process has a routine, rhythm and beat. Whilst strategy planning, customer insight research and the latest supply chain thinking will impact the budget process there are also human and organizational factors that will play a significant role.

A natural consequence of a crisis is that the level of uncertainty about the future from people inside and outside the company will rise and is likely to do so on all measures. What is the reaction of managers when this happens? My experience is that the re-forecasting of the budget can go into overdrive. I have watched the executive committees of large, international companies create mayhem in their local operating companies by asking the very reasonable question at every monthly board meeting: do we know where we are on the numbers for the full year? This request requires every country to reforecast its budget every month, involving not just finance, but all parts of the commercial operation. Managers are left with little time remaining to actually plan and take actions that could improve performance. Remember, when you ask for information there will always be a cost to the business.

The first question that you can ask is what is the purpose of the budget and does the existing way it is done deliver on that purpose? From this you can start to see how during the recovery period you can tune the budget process to deliver improved results. Introducing a whole new way of doing budgets is a time consuming and expensive project which, after a crisis, you may not be able to afford. However, better communication about the purpose and principles to be applied can be done quickly and cheaply.

For a publicly listed company one of the primary reasons that the business exists is to make a return for shareholders through dividends and increases in the share price. The share price is determined by the level of supply and demand for a share. This demand is driven by the various assumptions investors make about a company's future cash flows and is affected by any events that cause investors to change those assumptions. In most jurisdictions, a management team will have to inform the market if its latest projection of forecast outturn is significantly different from what the market expects – most normally in the form of a profits warning rather than a profits upgrade. At the very least you will need a budget process to ensure that you comply with these stock exchange regulations.

The more interesting question is whether the expectations of the market drive management to set the objectives for the budget or whether management uses the budget to set expectations with shareholders.

Let us assume that at Hypothetical Inc all of our leaders and managers behave in a rational manner, with no self-interest, and perfect judgement about future assumptions. The budget for the coming year is completed and shows an increase in net profits of 8 per cent. The investment analysts that follow Hypothetical Inc all have a forecast of at least 10 per cent growth in earnings. The choice for the leadership team is either to manage its investor communications to bring down consensus expectations to around 8 per cent or to push back on the internal budgeting process. The push back would ask the rational managers at Hypothetical Inc to 'up their game' and deliver a budget that achieved consensus market expectations. At the extremes two things could happen. The managers at Hypothetical Inc would become more innovative, ruthless and/or collaborative in order to plan the actions that would successfully deliver a higher level of earnings, without changing the structural risk profile of the company. At the other extreme, the managers plan projects and actions to deliver the higher numbers that do change the structural risk profile of the business. By a change in the structural risk profile I mean that managers start to do things to achieve the numbers that have a higher system-wide risk of failure than most shareholders would expect; for example, buying lottery tickets or making complex derivative bets on commodity movements. This type of behaviour results in a crisis in the end. As you look at your own budgeting process you can consider which of the two extremes at Hypothetical Inc your company is closer to.

The budget process should provide a clear link between equity and debt market expectations and internal targets. The promises to investors and lenders should be cascaded and shared around the wider senior management population so that they understand what the financial promises on the wobble board are. This provides a context for those managers to make commercial judgements and communicate to their teams. After a crisis there is an opportunity to rebase financial promises and to change the terms in which they are expressed. For example, promises and budgets which have a simple free cash flow generation objective give more 'self help' opportunities to managers than revenue or earnings targets. In uncertain times, missing a sales, or even a profit, target still allows a manager to use the levers of working capital, disposals and capital spending to deliver a cash flow promise.

Some last thoughts on the insights that can be gained from the budget process:

- A crisis may require a budget cycle to be performed in a shorter time period for a shorter forecast period. On day one you might have a matter of hours to do a budget for the next two weeks. The application of common sense and a simple spreadsheet can be very valuable at such times.
- Your managers and people know when leaders are asking them to do the impossible and you can lose credibility through the process very quickly.
- The flip side of this is that most people respond to a positive challenge where they have some opportunity to influence the outcome. Does the budget process tell people what to do or ask them what the targets could be and how they might deliver them?
- After a crisis, the wobble on the management board could be extreme. This requires you as a leader to provide simple, clear direction where possible and an authentic context. Try as hard as you can to make the budget objectives short in number, just two or three, and easy to understand.
- A difficult, and therefore mostly ignored, alternative to traditional budget processes is Zero Based Budgeting. This is discussed further in Chapter 7.

The forecast process

One of the most striking things about working in corporate restructuring for the last 15 years is the number of companies suffering a crisis that also had a total lack of a decent forecasting process. Huge efforts were put into the budget process and the monthly reporting of historic figures. The budget process itself was used for quarterly forecasting of full year outcomes, 3+9, 6+6 and 9+3 projections. However, an informed, regular and nimble process for updating forecasts of profit and cash flows was almost always missing. One of the first actions we would take after a crisis was to install weekly cash flow forecasting and a simple model to plug weekly sales numbers into reforecast profits, cash flows and covenant compliance for the current year. To buy more time with stakeholders we needed to talk about the future performance of the business, whereas the business systems and 90 per cent of the effort was often focused on recording and reporting historic financial information.

The other problem with many financial control systems is that they report from the recognition of financial revenues onwards. However, much of the insightful data that you want about future performance is contained in formal and informal customer management systems, like number of sales calls, outstanding proposals, invitations to tender and planned increases in government spending. A colleague of mine worked on a large restructuring of an automotive component supplier in North America at the start of the millennium. The sales forecasts were reviewed in detail over a period of five weeks for presentation to a syndicate of banks who had to decide whether to lend the company more money. Four days after management submitted the sales forecasts to the banks they had to go back and explain that the current year forecast that they had just handed over would be missed by over 30 per cent. The credibility of the management team was destroyed and my colleague had to spend huge amounts of time and skill in repairing the recovery plan. Why had management got the sales forecast so horribly wrong? The simplified answer was that they were asking the wrong people the questions about future orders, combined with a budget culture which had encouraged sales staff to hide bad news in the hope of things being OK in the end. The focus was on the accounting and not what was happening with customers.

We will discuss cash flow forecasting in more detail in Chapter 7. At this point it is worth remembering that forecasting is a skill the business can improve on with experience.

The more you do simple, regular forecasts of profits and cash flows and compare actual outcomes to your projections the better your business will become at forecasting. This opportunity to become more skilful at forecasting is a valuable one for a leader after a crisis.

Follow the money

The third viewpoint links very closely to the budget and forecast processes but also attempts to draw together a complete commercial and financial picture of the business. I repeat there is only one measure, cash, that brings together all of the aspects of a business. By definition, the free cash flow generated or absorbed by a company must include what is happening in sales, costs, tax, working capital, capital expenditure and debt and dividend payments. The objective here is to understand how cash flows into, through and out of the company. In doing so you will be able to challenge the 'sacred cows' and long held rules of thumb about how your company actually performs. This viewpoint is critical to a leader in stabilizing a business after a crisis and identifying the opportunities to build a viable recovery plan. Bluntly, if you do not understand cash you will not build a realistic and achievable recovery plan. Later in Chapter 7 we will examine the core business skill of cash management. At this stage there are two models I want to present, the $100 model and the value creation model used by Nestlé.

The $100 model is a simple tool that I have used on many restructurings and leadership development programmes I have run over the years. It is a test to see how well you and your senior management team understand how cash is created and absorbed in the business. The first stage should be straightforward. At a group level on the top half of a single piece of paper write down the following table for the latest 12 month period (see Figure 6.3).

	($)
Sales/revenue	100
Cost of goods sold	( )
Gross margin	
Operating costs	( )
Depreciation	( )
Interest costs	( )
Tax	( )
Profit/loss after tax	

Figure 6.3 The $100 model

Complete the table using your company's management or financial accounts. Taking revenue as always being $100 or 100 per cent, complete each line expressing the numbers effectively as percentages of sales for each of the lines to come down to a profit or loss after tax. For example, for a company with sales of $390 million, cost of goods sold of $230 million, operating costs of $109 million, depreciation of $16 million, interest costs of $19 million and tax of $12 million, the first part of the $100 model would be completed as in Figure 6.4.

	($)
Sales/revenue	100
Cost of goods sold	(59)
Gross margin	41
Operating costs	(28)
Depreciation	(4)
Interest costs	(5)
Tax	(3)
Profit/loss after tax	1

Figure 6.4 The $100 model

108 Turnaround leadership

What does this tell us? For the example above it shows that for every $100 of sales, the company makes $1 after tax profit. It also shows, simply, where the other $99 disappears to. Is this better than the last five years or the next forecast three years? How do competitors compare? Is the problem in volumes, pricing, cost structure, capital spending or capital structure?

On the second half of the same piece of paper, you will need to look at the cash changes in the business for each $100 of sales. Using the same example as above, the $390 million turnover company had the following cash movements in the same year:

- decrease in inventory of $20 million;
- increase in accounts receivable of $40 million;
- decrease in accounts payable of $35 million;
- capital expenditure of $25 million;
- debt raised of $40 million;
- dividends paid of $15 million.

This translates into the $100 table in Figure 6.5. Remember that the figures are expressed as a percentage of sales.

	($)
Profit/loss after tax	1
Add back depreciation	4
Decrease in inventory	5
Increase in accounts receivable	(10)
Decrease in accounts payable	(9)
Capital expenditure	(6)
Debt raised	10
Dividends paid	(4)
Decrease in free cash	(9)

Figure 6.5 The $100 model

So for our example company, $100 of sales has translated into a cash outflow of $9. In fact to cover the total $10 spent on capital expenditure and dividends we had to borrow the money from the bank.

Please remember the objective of the $100 model is to stir debate and raise questions, it is not an accounting exercise. In that context, what can the model really tell you? As a starting point ask yourself a few questions:

- How easy was it for you or your team to complete this exercise? Did it take 10 minutes for the CFO just using a flip chart and no notes or did it take half a day to produce?
- Were there a lot of arguments about definitions and criticism that the $100 model is too simplistic? At some level in the business I would suggest that the senior team need to share a 'simple' view of how cash is generated.
- Aside from the CFO, can each member of the executive committee complete the tables without referring to their finance colleagues for support? To be able to understand how your business can recover from a crisis I believe that all members of the senior team (sales, supply chain, operations, legal and support) need to be able to explain to the most junior manager how your business generates cash.
- Does everybody understand which way a change in working capital, for example a decrease in accounts receivable, impacts cash? When working with senior executives at international companies over 50 per cent of the non-financial managers make the wrong adjustment.

The point to be made is this. Unless the senior team has a shared basic understanding of the cash levers within your business then building and delivering a viable recovery plan is going to be difficult. My experience is that sophisticated discussions about brands, cost base optimization and cash management will be less valuable if the people around the board room table do not share a view about the basics of the business.

Once you have passed the first level of the $100 model then it opens up the possibility of a few more single sheets of paper. At a board level why not choose to ignore your complicated management information for an afternoon and look at:

- A $100 model for each of your operating units, comparing them in terms of cash usage and generation.
- The performance of the group and each operating unit on a $100 model over the last five years and the next three years according to your plan. This will ignore sales growth and focus on 'operating cash leverage'. Operating cash leverage is the change in the amount of cash you generate or forecast to generate from each $100 of revenue.
- If your systems allow it (if not, ask why) can you complete a $100 model by product, country or customer segment? There will be howls of protest about allocations and accounting treatments over this. On every restructuring I have worked on I was told this was not possible. It is. You have to remember that this is not an accounting exercise but an attempt to gain fresh insights. The battle you will have to generate the numbers is a valuable part of the education process for the senior leadership team.
- Make everybody watch the film *The Matrix*. At a point the hero of the film, Neo, sees through the fabric of the superficial nature of the computer-generated artificial world he is in to the underlying computer code behind it. To really understand your business, similarly to Neo, you need to see and feel how cash flows back and forth within it.

The real purpose of the $100 model is to make you step away from the detail of your existing management information. If your finance department says that it will take a week to produce the information then you have missed the point. This is about your collective understanding of the cash flow fundamentals of the business. Without this understanding you will be flying your recovery plan blind.

The second model to look at is more sophisticated but still related to the $100 model. Over a number of years Nestlé used an economic profit model to instruct its senior managers about how value is created for shareholders. The basic premise was that the free cash flow generated for investors on the capital invested in the business drove the value of the business. A higher free cash flow on the capital used would improve the return for shareholders. To make this real for managers in their day-to-day decisions about the business, Nestlé used a model of the key drivers that the leaders should focus on. There were seven key levers in the model:

1. sales growth;
2. profit margins;
3. working capital intensity;
4. fixed capital intensity;
5. income tax rate;
6. cost of capital;
7. value growth duration.

Each lever contributes to the overall free cash flow generation of the business and hence its valuation. An improvement in sales or margins will improve potential cash flow generation. However, the model reinforces that there are five other areas to consider in understanding cash generation. For each dollar of working capital improvement there will be an improvement in cash generated. The harder that the fixed assets can be worked, that is achieving more output from the same investment, the better the cash return. A lower tax rate and cost of money, the better the free cash flow. As valuation is based on future cash flows the last lever, value growth duration, considers how long you can sustain the business model that you have.

How can this model help you prepare a better recovery plan? As I keep saying, the two key resources that are in short supply after a crisis are time and cash. Being able to articulate to the key stakeholders how you will be able to generate cash by taking actions across each of these seven levers could buy you more time. The extra time that you have allows you to start to take actions around each lever to deliver improved cash generation. As you gather a deeper understanding of the business and the opportunities for a recovery, each lever provides you with a perspective to understand how the money flows in and out of your business.

In Chapter 7 we shall return to cash management as a core business skill to be mastered after a crisis.

Lean not mean

The fourth viewpoint to understanding the business after a crisis is the cost base. A crisis most often results in a fall in sales. That fall in sales might actually be the cause of the crisis and have been happening for a period of time prior to it reaching crisis point. Reference to previous economic downturns and 'bubble bursts' highlight a number of factors that can impact managers as sales start to decline:

1. Managers tend to be too slow and too optimistic in revising downwards the sales assumptions that they use in making decisions. The ability and speed of consumers and enterprises to 'do without' and spend less is often grossly underestimated by managers.
2. As customers adjust quickly to a more price conscious and cash limited world, managers are surprised when

new product and service offerings they perceive as having real, outstanding customer value and appeal, fail to take off.

3. This slowness to consider the scale and impact of changes in consumer and enterprise spending and behaviour puts managers on the back foot when reality turns out to be worse than their expectations. Options are reduced and blunt cost reduction measures are employed, mostly of the 'salami slicing' variety.

4. Coupled with a reluctance to rebalance the promises that have previously been made to investors, this can drive some managers to make increasingly harmful and risky decisions to deliver short-term targets and results and this tends to focus managers on internal issues and less on the customer. Paradoxically, this can reduce the range and scale of options available to the business to manage after a crisis. Seeing the world through the eyes of the consumer or enterprise can open up far more radical cost and margin improvement opportunities.

5. Managers may require exposure to new ways of working and tools and techniques to be able to find more radical solutions based on customer insights. This could include the application of customer-based lean thinking, the shift from 'good' to 'good enough' and low cost, consumer champion strategies.

6. Employees, suppliers, lenders and investors are all sensitive to the economic reality and any failure by management to acknowledge in their communications the change in conditions and the associated uncertainties can destroy trust in its credibility.

7. Each of the above reduces management's ability to set a realistic and compelling cost structure context for people to work within and make decisions against.

8. This failure to set an authentic context means that many companies miss out on the opportunity to capitalize on difficult market conditions.

To be able to break out of the vicious cycle of not taking cost base action fast enough requires a different approach to your cost base. Among the many tools that are available to a manager in setting the right cost base is Zero Based Budgeting (ZBB). One of the early books on this subject was by Peter Pyhrr (1977). Whilst this technique is applied to some extent by public sector organizations around the world, very few commercial businesses use it. The core of the tool is that each budgeting cycle assumes that all costs have to be re-justified. A set of scenarios of demand are developed and for each scenario the costs needed to stimulate and satisfy that level of demand are determined and only those costs are approved. It is a brutal, bottom-up process that most companies do not want to undertake every year. However, after a crisis it can be a valuable tool to consider.

The way I have used it on a restructuring after a crisis is to use the analogy of a food buffet. All the costs (people, property, external spend, IT, etc) are laid out on the buffet. The business unit leaders are then asked to select only the costs that they need to incur to deliver a particular level of demand from the buffet. They should not worry about legacy cost issues or long-term contractual agreements. Anything and anybody left on the buffet table in terms of costs will be dealt with by a separate cost reduction team that allows the commercial managers to focus on delivering the demand forecast with the cost base that they have selected. The exercise focuses on what are 'productive' costs and what are 'non-productive'. The outcome of the process is often that many difficult costs are left on the table. Also, investment needed to sustain a longer term competitive position can also sometimes be left on the table. The insight for you as a leader is the view of the commercial managers of what is absolutely necessary in terms of a cost base for a certain level of customer demand. After a crisis this can lead to new opportunities to identify realistic cost reductions.

One of the few commercial businesses that uses the ZBB approach is the brewer Anheuser Busch In-Bev, we mentioned in an earlier chapter. This company uses ZBB as a way of life for cost management, always trying to move each dollar of cost to the productive category. In my experience this is different from many corporate approaches to establishing a cost reduction 'programme'. A programme sets targets for cost reduction and has a start and an end. The ZBB approach looks at cost management as a never-ending way of life. The opportunity that a crisis gives you as a leader is to shift the mentality and ways of working of your business in many ways. One of those is to change the organization's approach to the productivity of the cost base. Perhaps by making cost management a way of life rather than a series of one-off programmes you can achieve that once in a lifetime change in the competitiveness of your company.

Flesh and blood

The penultimate viewpoint on your tour of the opportunities for the business after a crisis is to look at the company through the eyes of the human beings involved in it. Customers, bankers, investors, employees and suppliers are all people as well. Standing in the shoes of each of these stakeholders and understanding how they feel about the crisis and a potential recovery is an essential part of your work as a leader.

We can try to illustrate this with a few examples. A company that I advised in the technology sector, based in Continental Europe, suffered a massive fall in orders for its desktop computer servicing business over an 18-month period. We looked at the position from a product, demand and marketing perspective. We reviewed cash generation and cost reduction opportunities. Basically, the company had made the error of not moving from a 'break-fix' model of computer repair services to a complete solution for companies wanting functioning IT available for staff when and where they needed it. Other companies had moved into their market place offering a broader solution to IT delivery and maintenance whilst this company only provided people with screwdrivers to fix a broken laptop screen. Over the previous four years these types of break-fix services had grown significantly. The trouble was that they were also falling away just as fast as they had grown.

A critical part of the building of a recovery plan was to consider how all the people involved felt about the crisis. As there was a cash flow problem we could start with the financial stakeholders. The banks had lent money to the business one year previously based on a set of financial forecasts and assumptions about the market. The lead relationship banker had argued the case for lending the company money in front of the bank's credit committee. The historic growth in sales pointed to a very rosy future and the bank sanctioned a significant debt facility. When the reality of the fall in revenues became clear, the bank had a problem. But beyond the rational aspects of the problem, there was also a personal problem for the bank manager who had proposed the deal. He did not look very smart in the eyes of his colleagues. If the company ignored the personal feelings of the banker then we would not clearly understand how the bank might react. We had to consider how the person involved would think. After a crisis a bank may take control of a problem away from the original banker to a work-out department. In such a case a new banker will be handling the situation who not only did not do the original deal but also brings a fresh set of eyes to the situation. Once again, understanding this new person's perspective is critical in how a recovery plan is developed. A work-out banker (as in needing to 'work out' a problem) has a different approach to a situation than a relationship banker looking to generate new business. After a crisis have you stood in the shoes of your banks and felt how they are feeling?

I once attended a results presentation for an international manufacturing business we had, only two days previously, been engaged to help. I sat in the sixth row of the meeting with over 50 investment bank equity analysts attending. In front of me was the leading sell-side analyst for the sector from a major US bank. As the CEO stood up to start the presentation, the analyst in front of me turned to the person next to him, from a different bank, and whispered his view of the situation. The company had always been untrustworthy, would always be untrustworthy and nothing that they said today should be treated as credible. Except he actually used much more colourful language. Listening to this, I was shocked. I spoke to the corporate finance advisor to the company about it afterwards. He explained that 10 years previously the same, then junior, analyst had put out a strong buy recommendation on the company. A month later the management team had issued a major profits warning. That warning had cost the analyst credibility and a lower bonus that year. Despite the fact that an all new management team was now in place, the analyst would never forget or forgive the profits warning that happened a decade before.

Flesh and blood. Never forget the 'stakeholders' you need to give you the time and the money to deliver your recovery plan are also human beings. A lack of understanding about how people feel may be the vital missing element that prevents your recovery plan from being a success.

From an employee perspective this understanding is absolutely critical. From the senior team around the board room table to the clerk serving customers in a store, your recovery plan will be reliant upon your employees working harder, smarter and under conditions of increased uncertainty. On the flip side, the crisis may have been what many employees had been waiting for. A few years ago I advised a law firm with just over 90 staff and 18 partners. As with many professional services firms, the business was reliant upon a small number of the partners to generate the majority of fees from clients. There was a common understanding amongst most of the staff that at least five of the partners and 20 of the staff were being carried by the rest. The costs of 'carrying' these underperforming partners and staff eventually created a financial crisis. The bank refused to continue to extend the overdraft at the firm to pay partner drawings. Not much focuses a partner more than not being paid. The business was not in a bad location, it had some very good lawyers and clients and its focus on personal injury and associated litigation was a steady sector to be in. The problem was that almost 25 per cent of the people were not productive. Not only was this not efficient but it had the knock-on effect of lowering the overall morale of the people who were productive. After the crisis the recovery plan was clear. Either the non-productive staff and partners had to become productive or they had to leave. The much better solution was that they became productive, as this retained key skills and clients and was significantly cheaper in terms of redundancy costs. The opportunity to make them more productive was to publicize the effectiveness of each partner and lawyer.

Previously, there had been no real visibility on individual performance. Now, we published weekly on all the notice boards, including those in the tea rooms, how much each person had charged, billed and collected. The lists were ranked in terms of individual success. The impact was that if you were at the bottom of the list everybody, including the cleaner, knew it. Whilst quite a crude short-term incentive scheme, it had the desired effect. Of the 25 people that were unproductive, 12 of them were so annoyed at being shown up in public as being at the bottom of the tables that they changed their behaviours and improved their performance. Five of the lowest performers decided that they did not want to work in such an aggressive culture and voluntarily resigned, saving the firm the redundancy costs. The remaining eight people were eventually made redundant. As importantly as resolving the issue of the under-performers, the other productive staff felt that they were no longer having to carry other people and that the culture had become fairer.

I will give one last example of understanding how people feel as a tool to improve performance. The head of supply chain for a large drinks group in Europe explained how he dealt with a sickness absence problem with warehouse staff. The number of sick days was running at an astonishing 10 per cent of total days. A new statement went out from management to say that staff who had recently been absent through sickness would not be considered for overtime work. The company said it was concerned not to put the undue pressure of extra working on those people who had recently had to take time off through illness. Within one month of the new policy being implemented the absence rate through sickness was under 3 per cent.

Imagine new futures

The last viewpoint from which to complete a 360 degree insight into the business and the opportunities for a recovery is to consider how future trends and changes could impact the company.

As mentioned before, the positive side of a crisis is that it gives you as a leader the licence to make what could be a once-in-a-generation change to the business. If the crisis is one that has impacted everybody in your sector, for example a recession, then the opportunity should be even greater because all companies are under stress. In looking to future opportunities and threats it is important to consider how effective the company has been in the past at interpreting and responding to changes.

Remember that one of the drivers of a crisis we discussed in Chapter 4 was the lack of management sensitivity to change. If, to gain a fresh insight into the future after a crisis, you ask the same people the same questions as before, why will you generate any different answers?

In his book *Profiting from Uncertainty,* Paul Schoemaker (2002) explains the process of scenario planning. This tool is not about trying to predict the future. It is about constructing a range of possible versions of how the future might look. By understanding the range of possible futures, you can plan as to how you might profit in all circumstances. The point here is that you should be trying to understand the possible range of what the future might hold rather than trying to predict specific outcomes for the future.

Where can you go in order to understand the range of possible futures for your company and market? Having been a strategy director at a couple of companies, may I suggest you consult your strategic planning department last. Why? When I was in the strategy function we were possibly the function most removed from the coalface of the business. Our sources of insight were important: external consultancies, conferences, third party reports, competitor analysis. However, none of these were special sources of information unique to us. Everybody in the market was being sold the same ideas by McKinsey, Bain and the rest. What we really needed was sources of foresight that gave us a competitive advantage. One of the places to go searching for such foresights is within your own business. If you are going to look within the company how could you make the most of the efforts that you put in? There are three tools that you might consider using.

First, the 'your customer's customer' approach. One of the companies that has taken the real meaning of lean thinking, an obsession with customers rather than just supply chain tools, is the international logistics company Unipart. One of their many blue chip customers is Jaguar cars. They are responsible on a global basis for the sourcing, distribution and stock management of all of Jaguar's after-market spare parts. This includes the delivery of parts to every Jaguar dealer in the world. As well as being a world leader in lean thinking and people development, Unipart seek to know more about their customer's customer than their customer does. To be clear, this company considers that understanding the business and the customers of its own customers is an essential part of doing business. If I were running a strategy department today I think this is what I would focus them on.

The second tool if you are searching for some new ways to think about innovation, upcoming trends and design for customers is to use the IDEO Method Cards (2003). IDEO is a leading consultancy in the field of innovation and design. The Method Cards are a series of ideas about how a manager can better understand human needs and so design improved products and services to meet those needs. Ideas range from 'A Day in the Life' through 'Error Analysis' to 'Foreign Correspondents' and an 'Unfocus Group'. All of the Method Cards share the same philosophy, encouraging you to take new and more diverse viewpoints on the world to generate insights about your customers, employees and business.

One of the Method Cards relates to the third tool that you can use to think about the future; asking the right questions. A card describes the 'Five Whys?' approach that was promoted as part of the Toyota Production System by Taiicho Ohno. The Five Whys? exercise makes the questioner ask 'why?' questions in response to five consecutive answers. The idea is that each 'why?' question digs a bit deeper into the underlying cause of a particular problem. This is one example of how the type of question you ask will determine the quality of the insights you generate.

When thinking about the future after a crisis you may often need to convince people that you actually have a future. To help lead people through the recovery plan it will be necessary to provide them with a sense of purpose about the future. A version of the ancient saying 'without a vision the people perish' can be applied to a business crisis. The crisis will often have weakened people's faith and commitment to the existing vision or purpose of the business. As part of the recovery plan you will need, one step at a time, either to create a new purpose or rebuild a modified version of the original purpose of the business.

For example, I worked with the new CEO of the international maternity and baby retailer Mothercare. My role was limited to the cash stabilization work necessary to provide a sound financial footing for the plans that the new CEO had for the business. When he took over in 2002 the business had given four profits warnings in under a year. The media and financial commentators were questioning the very role and existence of the business. The recovery plan implemented by the new CEO focused external commentators on the priorities of fixing the basics of the business, including logistics, products, customer service and trading. In addition, however, the new leadership team also started to create an additional purpose for itself and vision of what its future could hold. A small existing international operation was expanded via franchising so that by 2009 the company had over 1,000 stores in over 50 countries. A company that was seen as principally a single country operation has created an international purpose for itself. Since 2002 the value of the company has increased fivefold.

Next steps

This is the second area of the five aspects of leadership expertise that could help you recover successfully from a crisis.

The natural human reaction is to take action. We will talk about how to do this in the next four chapters. However, action without insight and foresight might lead you to a worse position than you are already in following a crisis. Always take some time to think and reflect.

7 Core business skills 1 – cash and time

The third area of leadership expertise is developing the core business skills that could help you deliver a successful recovery plan. Most of these skills will be familiar to you based on your existing business experience. Some will be more practised than others. The purpose of this chapter is to help you develop those areas that you have less experience in and to fine tune those where you have more expertise, for a post crisis situation.

The core business skills that we look at are:

- managing cash flow and time;
- developing strategy after a crisis;
- maintaining sales;
- cost base restructuring.

As previously discussed the two resources most in short supply after a crisis are time and cash – and these are closely related. We will look at the last three skills in Chapter 8, although each of the other areas of core business skills all feed back into the problems of generating more time and cash for your recovery plan.

Managing cash flow and time

Even companies not facing a crisis should always be trying to improve the amount of free cash flow they generate from their business operating model. An improvement in free cash flow generation improves the valuation of a company and the opportunities it has to make strategic and tactical choices. To achieve this, initiatives will be undertaken around customer payment terms, how many days payment suppliers will extend, stock management, capital spending schedules and debt repayment profiles. In a crisis, however, these types of activities can take on a whole new impetus. If your crisis has generated a cash flow issue, how do you take your focus on cash to a new level?

There is an unhappy truth to be uncovered. My experience is that the majority of companies do not understand how cash is generated and used within their business at a sufficient level of detail. Gaining this understanding at the right level of granularity is not a priority for most businesses in stable times. Innovation, market share growth, operating leverage and M&A take a much higher priority. By the way, in a stable environment it is possible to argue that this is the right thing to do. Understanding cash at a granular level is a difficult and time consuming thing to do and resources could well be better spent on other activities. For some companies the journey to understand cash as an essential KPI within their business only happens after a crisis and sometimes not even then. I apologize for spending so much time on this before we discuss the tools and techniques but this is an important mind shift that you might have to make. Understanding cash as a platform to gain fundamental insights into your business after, or even before, a crisis calls for an active change in leadership and management philosophy.

Ram Charan writes insightfully about the need for a leader's deep understanding of cash in his books *What the CEO Wants You to Know* (2001) and *What the Customer Wants You to Know* (2008). Both books are essential reading for any business leader. He describes the concept of 'velocity', which in corporate restructuring we have long been using in the context of 'cash velocity'. Cash velocity is the speed with which an idea or concept is converted into cash. It is also an important part of 'cash conversion'. Cash conversion is the percentage of sales and capital spending that is turned into cash that the business can keep. Charan describes in his books how a market stall trader fundamentally understands cash. I will use a similar story from a CEO I worked with who had not read either of Charan's books but understood the principles completely.

This CEO would describe to his fellow directors, managers and front line workers the tale of a market stall holder selling oranges in a small town in Yorkshire, England. To prosper, this market trader needed to have the cash to buy the oranges from wholesalers at the beginning of the day. That outlay of cash had to be converted into more cash by the end of the day if he was to buy stock for the next day, pay the rent of the stall, make a profit, feed his family and satisfy the tax man. There was no need for complicated accounting or management information systems. The cash at the end of the day would clearly determine success or otherwise. It seems that once a business becomes a certain size this fundamental insight into cash as the determinant of success or otherwise becomes lost.

A small business owner will focus on cash. A large organization leaves cash to its treasury function. Something becomes lost in this transition.

How can you restore this understanding of cash in a large organization? My experience is that there is a tool available to do this, but it is so painful to the DNA of a large business that most will not use it. That is until a crisis strikes and gives you the opportunity to implement it. Many management teams will still not use the tool even when they need it most after a crisis. Why? Because it requires senior leaders to engage in a cross-functional process which will expose the fact that they might not control and understand the business as well as they thought.

You are probably now waiting for a miraculous though possibly painful solution to your cash flow problems. Unfortunately, the solution is rather mundane. When experienced turnaround or restructuring professionals take over after a crisis the first thing that they instigate is a cash flow forecast. Exciting or what? The first forecast is likely to be for a 13-week period. We will discuss the steps necessary to produce a rolling cash flow forecast below. However, firstly it is important to discuss why a cash flow forecast can help you gain insight into your business and control after a crisis. To prepare a cash flow forecast for the next 13 weeks will require managers across the business to speak to each other. When will a sale be made? When will it be invoiced? When will it be paid? When will a supplier make a delivery? When will they require payment? When will we actually pay them?

For the first forecast managers will use their previous experience and understanding of how they think the business generates cash together with what they will also think is a lot of effort to produce a cash forecast. The next step is for the executive board to review the forecast against actual cash flow for the first week. As this is only a week's forecast the actual result should not be too distant from the forecast. Actually, in most cases the gap between the forecast and actual cash flows even for the first week can be significant. As each week goes by the accuracy of the first forecast produced will normally be shown to be very poor. Three very positive things should flow from this lack of accuracy, provided you adopt the right attitude to the insights that cash flow forecasting can bring.

First, explore the reasons why there is a difference between the forecast cash flow and the actual. Each week there will be many reasons why there is a difference. Understanding each of the reasons provides an opportunity. The opportunity will be to understand how the business actually operates and how to make an improvement in the cash flow velocity. For example, many budgets allocate costs evenly over a year for the purposes of reporting profits. In reality, many costs are not paid for in cash evenly over the year. For example, insurance premiums are often paid annually in advance. This might seem a simple example that surely most managers would know. My experience is that this is not true, especially in larger organizations. Each little opportunity to improve cash velocity and cash conversion makes the business more effective and resilient to the types of shocks that cause a crisis. You can continue the forecasting and review period for at least six months and still be gathering new, multiple opportunities to improve your business. This is not a silver bullet – the mythical business solution that radically improves performance with a simple, single set of actions. The cash flow and review process is a continual source of improvements, which in my experience is a hugely valuable tool for a business.

Second, the poor set of results of actual cash flow versus forecast should provide a platform for you to realign management's focus and humility. A number of crises occur because business leaders lose touch with the essence of their business and believe too much in their own public relations. Witness what happened to major banks around the world that required state handouts to survive after the credit crisis, following a decade of what turned out to be reckless expansion. If your senior management team cannot even forecast cash flow in the business for the next three months without a reasonable degree of accuracy, perhaps they should focus on business fundamentals until they can. A focus on fundamentals is often a good strategy after a crisis.

Third, after a crisis your financial stakeholders will expect you to be, and to be seen to be, in total control of cash. The disappointment of your first few sets of cash flow forecasts should motivate you and your team to radically improve the capability of the business to understand how, where and when cash is used and generated. Consistently producing poor quality cash flow forecasts that you have to share with your banks will not buy you the extra time you need after a crisis.

These three benefits all link into one extra benefit you can gain from mastering cash flow forecasting and review. All of the three benefits above require the business to operate and collaborate more effectively on a cross-functional basis. The goal of improved cross-functional working is cited as a key strategic priority for many organizations. It is meant to open up more opportunities for innovation, customer service and cost reduction. I have seen a number of cultural change programmes being designed to encourage and facilitate improved cross-functional working. Some of them failed because they were poorly conceived and implemented, without the right level of executive sponsorship. However, many failed because the wrong key performance indicators were used. Cash is not only a true cross-functional KPI, it is the only one that brings together all of the aspects of the business – sales, costs, tax, working capital, capital expenditure, financing and capital structure. If you want to use improved cross-functional working to deliver a successful recovery plan, using cash as a platform for change might be a good place to start.

The last thing to say to try to motivate you to make cash a strategic board level issue, especially after a crisis, is that it gives you access to the other resource that is in short supply after a crisis – time. Financial stakeholders will be more likely to provide the support and restraint required for you to build a recovery plan and deliver it if they consider that you and the senior management team are masters of cash and cash flow forecasting.

We will next turn to some specific cash forecasting and management tools. The areas covered are:

- cash committee;
- forecasting;
- time and cash before the accounting starts;
- cash improvement opportunities;
- trapped cash;
- capital spending;
- working capital.

All of these tools have multiple purposes: improved cash generation, buying more time for your recovery plan, re-engaging management with the detail of the business and creating stakeholder confidence that you are in control.

Cash committee

Because a focus on cash is an excellent way to generate better cross-functional thinking and working, one of the first steps after a crisis is to establish a cash committee. The committee is responsible for producing the cash flow forecasts and planning and monitoring cash improvement initiatives. In order to be effective, members should be senior representatives from across sales, operations, IT, finance and treasury and it should not be accountable to the treasury function. The committee should report to the executive committee and be chaired by the finance director. The key tasks will be to:

- establish the opening cash positions;
- establish financial creditor commitments;
- prepare short-term cash flow forecasts;
- review actual results with forecasts on a weekly basis;
- prepare a weekly report for the executive on the forecast and reasons for any differences;
- identify improvement opportunities based on the gaps identified;
- establish targets for the business for cash flow generation, velocity and conversion;
- be the programme office for wider cash initiatives, such as a cash race.

Cash committees are only helpful to the business and to you as a leader, when they have the right level of sponsorship and attention from the executive committee and the board.

The first two tasks on the list are critical to ensuring that the forecasts are based on a correct starting point and the promises to lenders are clearly understood. One of the partners I worked with in restructuring would take an obsessive interest in whether the opening cash position of the business we were working with was correct. This became known as the 'Wheeler Test'. A business that has not previously suffered a liquidity crisis will often not take the routine care to ensure that the opening cash positions used in its financial forecasts are completely accurate. Sometimes the reconciliations of amounts in the cashbook to the bank account statements have not been routinely completed. It is very embarrassing and costly in terms of credibility, and therefore available time, to have to restate the opening cash positions. A banker is not likely to be sympathetic towards a management team that does not even know how much cash it has. I commend the Wheeler Test to your cash committee as a good place to start.

The other critical starting task for the committee is to have a central and complete analysis of the banking and funding facilities the business has. What and where are the committed and uncommitted finance lines, the letters of credit, bonding lines, credit insurance arrangements and cash pools? What are the critical terms of these facilities, such as covenant levels for interest or asset coverage, cross-default provisions and inter-company guarantees? In a liquidity crisis the business must understand the minefield of promises it has made to its creditors. In 8 out of 10 cases I have worked on, a central and complete record of such promises has not existed when we were first engaged.

Forecasting

If the crisis you are facing has generated liquidity problems, then cash flow forecasting is going to be an essential skill for you and the business to master. There are basically two types of forecasts. A short term, 13-week forecast driven from your balance sheet and an 18-month to three-year forecast driven by your profit and loss account assumptions about the future.

For the short-term forecast to be reliable it needs to be based on your balance sheet. This is termed a 'receipts and payments' cash flow. A receipts and payments (R&P) cash flow forecast takes the opening position of your cash, accounts receivable and payable and unwinds them, week by week over the 13-week period. A simplified pro forma R&P cash flow would look like Figure 7.1.

	Week 1	Week 2	[ ]	Week 13
Receipts				
Accounts receivable				
Cash sales				
Total				
Payments				
Tax				
Accounts payable				
Payroll				
Interest/debt repayment				
Total				
Opening cash/overdraft				
Closing cash/overdraft				
Bank overdraft limit				
Headroom				

Figure 7.1 Receipts and payments cash flow

The receipts section analyses line-by-line when you expect to receive payments from customers or other sources. The cash committee will need to engage with sales, operations and accounts to determine this with accuracy. New sales still to be made and the money that can be collected from them during the period will have to be forecast and will obviously be based upon assumptions. Differences in the assumptions made between functions will start to cast some light on how cash actually flows in the business as opposed to how some managers think it flows.

On the payments lines the forecast needs to unwind the amounts and timing of payments due to trade creditors, tax authorities, finance providers (interest and capital), employees and other creditors. Once again, this requires you to look into every corner of the business and dispel some of the myths about how and when people are paid. It is not uncommon to find payments being made to suppliers earlier than the agreed terms because of historic practice or convenience.

The net weekly inflow or outflow of cash is then set against the opening cash or overdraft position and a closing cash position established. This is then compared to the available funding from lenders and a headroom position established. This headroom forecast over a 13-week period starts to identify where the pinch points in the cash position will be. Remember to adjust the available funding line to reflect facilities that are due for renewal. Can you assume that maturing facilities will be renewed?

This short-term forecast is then reviewed each week against actual cash flows. The differences are your source of fresh insight into your business.

The 18-month, or longer, cash forecast is normally based on your projections of sales, costs, working capital, tax and capital spending, debt and dividend payments and acquisitions or disposals. As such it will embody the essence of your recovery plan in a financial form. It will also contain lots of assumptions about the future and, as I have stressed throughout this book, the care taken with these assumptions is an essential part of rebuilding trust with your stakeholders after a crisis.

Time and cash before the accounting starts

Before we look at some of the areas of opportunity to improve cash velocity and conversion we should consider the vast area for possible improvement that does not show up on the financial statements. When most companies think about cash flow management they consider how to improve payments from customers and delay outflows to suppliers. The focus is on improving what is already shown up in the accounts. In addition to this is the time, and therefore cash velocity opportunity, that occurs before any records are made in the accounts. This is about your business velocity. How fast can you take an idea, turn it into a saleable product or service, attract a customer and convert this into an order? Clearly the shorter the time it takes from idea to invoice the faster you will generate cash. Of course it is essential to improve your order to cash cycle but it is also possible to improve your idea to order time.

A car manufacturer will spend billions on the research and development for a new model, the advertising launch, dealer training and initial production before a car is ever sold. Think of this in terms of cash velocity. The salary paid to an engineer working on a new model may not see a cash return in terms of a customer order and payment for many years. The cash for that salary cheque may be 'unproductive' from a cash perspective for a very long time. This can be compensated for on an accounting treatment basis by capitalizing the costs and spreading them over the years that the new model is actually sold but it does not change the fact that the cash has been spent years before any cash is received in return. The issue is about shortening the time between idea and customer order.

As well as product development there is also the cash spent in marketing and securing an order. The time taken from meeting a new customer to signing an order can also be a fertile area for improving cash velocity that just does not always appear on the financial KPIs. For example, I worked with a small engineering business that makes specialist prototypes for design companies. The advent of new technology has allowed them to change their business model, reduce costs and radically improve cash velocity and conversion. Historically, they had 10 sales representatives on the road in Europe seeing potential customers, costing over $2 million a year to run. Once a potential customer had been identified, drawings would be discussed, a price determined and then the drawings converted into detailed specifications that could be used by the machinists to produce a model. On average, the time taken from finding a potential customer to producing an order in the factory took six months. Not only was this process expensive, it was also a very slow cash return on the money paid to the sales representatives. Two changes in technology allowed the business to restructure itself radically. The development of computer aided design software allowed drawings to be downloaded electronically directly from the software to the machines making the prototypes and Google changed the way that new customers could be found. Today, the company carefully controls its spend on customer acquisition through the amount it commits to Google for presence on internet searches relating to the production of prototypes. The flexibility of the Google marketing tool allows the management to manipulate its advertising spend. Customers now seek out the company after a Google search, so all enquiries now come from there. The business no longer has any sales representatives and saves the $2 million a year, less the $500,000 paid out to Google. When an enquiry arrives it is in the form of a download from a computer aided design package which can be instantly sent through to a machine for production. The added value is in having engineers in-house who can adapt the design to meet the constraints imposed by the materials used. From a cash velocity perspective the money spent with Google each month produces orders the same month. The business now has more sales, better margins, improved customer service and a much healthier cash flow.

Opportunities for cash flow improvement outside the traditional accounting records need not only come from better management of the sales function. I spent some time in Japan visiting and researching companies that applied lean thinking to their business, a subject we will return to in the next chapter. One example that is relevant to cash velocity is how one of the companies worked with its suppliers. The normal practice of just-in-time delivery was being applied so only the materials required for immediate production were ordered and delivered and cash outlays were reduced. But the company had also established a relationship with its suppliers to reduce the combined cash cycle time of both their businesses that included helping their suppliers apply lean thinking within their own supply chains. Most importantly, the company recognized that many of its suppliers bought from the same manufacturers that it also bought from and pooled the buying activities and purchasing power of all its suppliers with its own. Through this combination all of the suppliers were able to secure better prices and enhanced payment terms and the benefits shared between the company and its suppliers, although not on an entirely equal basis!

So, as you start to think about improving cash flow as part of your recovery plan, you should always consider opportunities that lie beyond the immediate areas of working capital as shown in the accounts.

Cash improvement opportunities

We can now turn to the more traditional opportunities to improve cash flow such as trapped cash, capital spending and working capital. In addition, there are a few other areas to consider as well.

For most companies one of the largest areas of cash outflow is in the form of sales taxes, corporation tax and employee-related taxes. In each of these areas local rules and regulations can be investigated to determine opportunities for cash flow benefits. For example, in some jurisdictions the sales taxes or value added taxes can be paid either on an accruals basis or a cash accounting basis. The cash paid in tax on an accruals basis is calculated based on invoices sent to customers and received from suppliers. This does not reflect when the cash is actually paid by customers or by you to suppliers. If customers pay a long time after the invoice is sent, a company might have to pay over the sales tax before receiving the amount due. On a cash accounting basis the tax is only paid when it is received from customers. A change in methodology can sometimes generate a welcome one-off cash flow gain.

Financing cash flows might also be an area of opportunity. Invoice discounting or factoring can have its benefits but can also be difficult to arrange after a crisis. Asset-backed financing provides security to a lender from the company's assets rather than its overall business. Sale and leaseback of property or capital assets might also provide a necessary short-term cash flow boost but at the expense of longer-term cost or loss of flexibility. After a crisis it may be necessary to take some actions to secure a future which in healthier times you would not have considered.

This thought also applies to disposals. A director of an airline business I was advising asked me why they were selling off the profitable parts of the business after a crisis, to generate much needed short-term cash flow. The answer was rather bland; they were the only parts that anyone would buy at that point and without the money the group as a whole would fail. Sometimes, after careful thought and consideration of the alternatives, selling some of the family silver might be the only way to secure the time to rebuild the rest of the business.

Trapped cash

One of the first places to look for additional cash after a crisis is cash trapped in parts of the business that could be better applied elsewhere within the group. Once a company reaches a certain size of operations and geographic coverage there will be a need to ensure that the day-to-day working of local companies can be efficiently carried out. Over time, and in the absence of a cash crisis, this can lead to cash being 'trapped' within the organization and not available where it is needed after a crisis. I worked with a building supplies business with operations across 20 countries. The group operated with a requirement for a minimum of $50 million in its group cash pool. If it dipped below the $50 million level then it would face severe financing issues with its group of 20 lending banks. The company would have to go back to those banks and ask for new facilities to top up its available headroom. After falling sales created a crisis in the business, the company was dangerously close to its limits. A renegotiation would be painful and expensive. Within the local operations, over the years the country managers and accountants had been using local banking facilities for trading that fell outside the group's cash pooling arrangements. In addition, local managers had become accustomed to keeping some extra cash for a rainy day and none of this locally held cash was available at a group level. There were also some system and structural reasons why not all of the local cash was making its way into the group's pooled cash resources. A lot of detailed work on policies, better communication and a few system changes released $35 million of previously trapped local cash to flow into the group cash pool within a two-month period. The only impact on local operations was they had to pay closer attention to forecasting and cash management, which was actually a benefit.

In a retail business I advised, the trapped cash was nothing more complex than that they were holding too much cash in the tills as a float. A 20 per cent reduction in the float carried by each store produced $3 million of extra cash at a group level. This attention to detail about cash resulted in the company not having to increase its borrowings at a time when the banks had major concerns about lending it any more money. In fact, the bankers were impressed with the new management's focus on producing cash from within the business rather than asking them for more money.

Capital spending

One of the major areas of cash commitment is on capital items such as property, IT and plant and machinery. After a crisis this spending will almost certainly have to be reviewed and often reduced for a period of time. There are two ways to approach the issue of capital investment. First, what can be afforded? Second, what does the recovery plan require? There will often be a difference between the two approaches, especially at the start of the recovery plan, immediately after the crisis. In addition, some of the future capital spending may already be contractually committed.

Both approaches can benefit from the application of zero based budgeting, 'ZBB', which I have already described. This approach starts by considering some scenarios of future customer demand. A crisis that has been brought about through a recession will require those scenarios to be brutally realistic about when, and to what level, demand will return. Within those scenarios all capital spending must be justified on an item by item basis. It is not sufficient, for example, to argue that maintenance capital spending has always been 5 per cent of sales. Every operator within the business will consider that their investment plans are sacrosanct and the use of 'maintenance spending' as a justification for approval is a way of gaining funds. As a leader using a ZBB approach you need to ensure that a fundamental root and branch review is undertaken.

Working capital

This is the area most traditionally associated with cash flow management. It contains three different components all requiring individual approaches, accounts receivable, accounts payable and work-in-progress and inventory. Before going into each area it is worth standing back and thinking about working capital as a whole. The structure of your working capital needs reflects the business operating model you have. In fact, it is a result of the strategy that you have for the business, although not often a focus of a strategy development process. Whilst tactical and operational improvements in the management of working capital are a critical element of better cash management, radical changes in working capital come about because of changes in the business model. After a crisis you may have the opportunity to change the strategic nature of your investment in working capital.

One of the biggest changes in working capital structures has been as a result of consumer self-service, low cost, operating models. When you log on to the internet to book airline, hotel or car rental purchases, you are often driven by a 'buy early for the lowest fares' incentive. While you may have gained a bargain by buying early, you are almost always required to pay your cash over at the point of purchase. This can be months before you use the purchase. The airline does not have to pay for its aviation fuel until a few days after your actual flight departs but you have paid over the ticket price, say, four months previously. The airline's operating model has a positive effect on its working capital. Why not buy a full tank of fuel for your hire car in advance? It saves the excess refuelling charges on return. The car hire company has the benefit of your cash in advance and it knows that you are unlikely to return the car with a completely empty fuel tank. Double bonus. Even coffee shops understand this. Pick up a pre-paid card to gain the convenience of not having to have the cash to pay for your coffee and we will reward you with a free coffee for every 10 purchases. Not only does the coffee shop tie you in to making purchases from them but they also receive your cash before you have had your coffee.

After a crisis many customers will have concerns about buying from you. If you can provide them with additional perceived benefits and change the cash profile of your working capital investment at the same time, then you are starting to build a robust recovery plan.

Accounts receivable

This is the money that customers owe you for the goods or services that they have received. In some sectors, like retail, you receive the majority of that cash at the point of purchase. But, taking the example of the coffee shop pre-paid cards, you can still make cash flow improvements in a retail environment. In the majority of other businesses you will be providing some form of credit to your customers. Improving this order to cash cycle has attracted an extensive range of ideas and I do not propose to set out the approaches that are well covered elsewhere. Rather we can ask some questions about how you approach accounts receivables after a crisis. The normal things to consider are:

- speeding up the sending out of invoices;
- invoicing some items earlier than others;
- fast tracking disputed invoices;
- offering an early settlement discount;
- offering an alternative to a settlement discount for earlier payment, for example enhanced service;
- changing and accelerating the banking process you use to collect cash from credit card providers.

There are two additional things to think about apart from process improvement and the business model changes discussed above. One of the tasks of the cash committee should be to bring together all the parts of the business that secure a sale, set the payment terms, deliver the product or service and do the accounts processing. Sales, marketing, legal, operations, IT and finance need to work together to squeeze every day out of the cycle of invoicing and cash collection.

The second action is to give customers a good reason to pay you before others. A trade supply business I worked with gave immense freedom to its local managers to set price, service and local policies. Payment and debt collection policies were, however, handled centrally, giving the local manager absolutely no influence on payment terms. Neither was the central team given any latitude on late payment, not even if the customer was the owner's brother! Because the product supplied was good, well priced and always available, the tradesman relied upon this business to be able to do his work. At the end of the month the tradesman might have 15 different invoices to pay but not enough money to pay all of them. This company, he knew, did not ever extend extra credit terms and he needed their product next month to complete jobs and be paid himself. Therefore, he would always ensure that he paid that bill first. Put yourself in the shoes of your customer when they are deciding which bills to pay at the end of the month. How do you ensure that your invoice is at the top?

Accounts payable

Now the shoe is on the other foot. Your suppliers are one of the four key stakeholders we have talked about to whom you make promises when standing on your leadership wobble board. My view is that, unless you are in a position to dominate your suppliers, it is best, after a crisis, to take a constructive attitude to them. A positive approach to your essential suppliers, emphasizing a longer-term partnership, could be better than just trying to beat them up. A thoughtful strategy based on an insight into what each supplier might require could open the door to more creative solutions. One technology company I worked with used an 'Intel inside' approach to gain better payment terms. By agreeing to acknowledge the supplier's intellectual property visibly on our end product we secured an additional 60 days credit. The supplier was cash rich but had the strategic priority of raising its brand awareness. Our understanding of that enabled a different style of conversation with the supplier.

Most likely though, if you are facing a liquidity crisis you will have to try to extend payment terms to suppliers. For commodity suppliers where you can substitute easily you can take one approach. For more strategic suppliers, care will be required. One vital point to consider is credit insurance companies. Many of your suppliers will have insured your debt to them. The insurer will pay out if you default on payment. The insurer therefore has an active interest in the health of the companies its customers are supplying. If you do not engage with these insurers and unilaterally extend your suppliers' payment terms you run the risk of the insurer reducing or removing the cover. This is often the trigger that causes a trading and liquidity crisis for a company.

Inventory and work-in-progress

The last aspect of working capital management is inventory or stock and work-in-progress. This returns us to the question of cash velocity. Money tied up in inventory is necessary dead money. You cannot fulfil customer promises without some stock. The question is how much cash do you need to tie up in inventory to meet the promises you have made? As with our discussions about other areas of working capital I do not intend to delve into the hundreds of techniques available for making tactical improvements to inventory management and cash velocity. Every company and industry is different in the approaches it can take to improve inventory turn. Instead I want to ask the rather academic question – what is the purpose of inventory? As you fight your way out of a crisis you have the opportunity to consider the purpose of inventory in your business. The CEO of a retail chain once told me the accountants had categorized stock on the wrong side of the balance sheet – it was a liability not an asset.

Let us start this discussion in the automobile sector. I remember a story told to me by a specialist consultant, and I apologize if it is not wholly accurate or I am attributing the original story to the wrong person, but it still makes a point. He told me that a CEO of one of the big three US car makers had said that he would always discount his cars in order to keep his factories at full production. The CEO of a rival European car manufacturer swore that he would shut every factory before discounting his cars. A possible explanation for this diversity of views is the horrors of inventory accounting. Every car that is made is valued in the accounts as including the raw materials to make the vehicle and a proportion of the manufacturing overheads. Even if none of the cars being made will ever be sold, they will sit in the balance sheet having absorbed costs that do not, in that period, have to be recognized in the profit and loss account. But, from a cash perspective this accounting treatment does not make any difference. You still have to pay the workers' wages, heat, light and electricity that month, even if the cars are sitting unsold in a field. The accounting treatment drove certain management actions, tied up cash, but did not address the fundamental problems in the business. If you are continually being forced to discount stock, and not as part of a thought-through business strategy, you should really be asking some big questions about your operating model. Even worse, if you don't discount your stock to realize sales and cash and instead have obsolete, ageing stock around the business you are heading for a bigger crisis.

Back to the question – why do companies have inventory? Given the trillions of dollars tied up in stock around the world there must be a very good reason. The value you can add to your business in its recovery phase is to ask why you have inventory in your business.

If it were possible, either via technology or magic, to create the inventory for a customer at the point they require it then nobody would hold stock. We would release the trillions of dollars tied up in inventory as free cash flow. Just look at the change to digital download of music, film and literature content that renders producing physical CDs, DVDs and books less relevant and unproductive from a cash flow perspective. iTunes is a big music store but it does not have any cash tied up in physical stock. So what are the possible reasons for holding inventory?

- Stock has to be available, on-hand, to make the sale. A grocer needs to have oranges on the shelf for customers to buy.
- It is cheaper to make inventory in batches and suffer the cash flow penalty of having stock, warehouses and supply chain infrastructure. We are trading margin for cash consumption.
- The inventory is a fire-break against variable customer demand that allows service levels to be maintained.
- The business has always operated with a certain level of stock.

Let me make it clear, in most businesses that hold stock I do not believe that inventory can be eliminated. I am just asking you the question why you hold the amount of stock that you do. This is real, valuable cash tied up in the inventory that could be vital to the success of your recovery plan.

My experience is that the level of inventory in a business is driven by five factors: the customers you choose to serve; the geography of your business; the product range you offer; the legacy assets that you have in production and supply chain, and the ingrained assumptions your management team has about how the business should operate. The first four can be subject to analysis, consultant advice and aspects of lean production. The last one is a leadership issue you have the opportunity to address after a crisis.

Cash, cash, cash and time

If your crisis has generated a liquidity problem, and, maybe, even if it has not, cash management is a critical skill for a turnaround leader. It builds credibility with stakeholders and buys you more time. Remember, time and cash are often your most precious resources.

8 Core business skills 2

This second chapter on the core business skills to develop to help you design and deliver a better recovery plan focuses on the following areas:

- developing strategy after a crisis;
- maintaining sales;
- cost base restructuring.

Assuming that your continuing management of the cash flow position of the business provides the time to consider a more detailed, medium-term recovery plan, you need to start to make some choices about the business and how it will be run. In Chapter 9 we will refer to the sources of new ideas and possibilities for your business operating model. In Chapter 6 we looked at how to take a 360 degree view of your company and its market. Both of these chapters should provide you with some thoughts and ideas about how to start to build a better business after a crisis. The three areas of core business skills examined below are really about ensuring you have a balanced set of skills and expertise to apply to the problems you are facing. A business leader in a turnaround situation needs a broad range of expertise and insights. While you cannot be expected to have expertise in every area, removing one's blind spots and establishing a minimum level of competence are, I believe, valuable steps in leadership development.

What we can cover in each of the three areas will not be sufficient to establish the level of competence you need for your particular circumstances. Rather, it should help you identify areas of concern for you and that you will want either to do more development work on or ensure your team as a whole has the expertise it needs.

Before turning to each of the three areas we ought also to consider the bigger question of whether you should start on the journey towards using an overarching management system to run the company in the future. I would argue that most companies do not adopt a systematic approach to management but rather run things using a collection of management ideas and ad hoc styles. There are, of course, companies that do apply a system, either one they have developed themselves or an 'off-the-shelf' solution that has been tailored to the individual business.

Examples of complete and partial management systems would include the Toyota Production System, applied by others as lean thinking, Six Sigma, total quality management and the balanced scorecard. Some companies have been developing their 'way' of doing business for decades. The advantage of a systematic approach is that it can accelerate the design and implementation of change by providing ready-made tools and solutions. The risk is that the system is used as a substitute for the business insights that are relevant to a particular company's position.

While recognizing that all of these systems have their supporters and each has merits, I do think that, after a crisis, there are aspects of the lean thinking approach that can be highly applicable:

- It is a system that, if done properly, places the customer at the core of the business.
- The tools used seek to give power and capability into the hands of the people who are closest to the coalface.
- It focuses on step changes and the sustaining power of continuous improvement.
- Visual communication is an essential part of the philosophy, and this helps with monitoring and early warnings of problems ahead.
- The focus on eliminating waste is a good place to start after a crisis.

I have worked with CEOs who considered that the lean approach somehow devalues their management flexibility or is just an issue for manufacturing and supply chain. If this is the case in your company I would not bother with lean as a tool. Without the right level of executive sponsorship it can become an expensive distraction.

Developing strategy after a crisis

After the initial stabilization phase following a crisis, when sufficient time has been secured to consider the medium-term future of the business, you will have to start to develop a future strategy for the company. This becomes important as people start to emerge from the bunkers to see what the future potential of the business could be. Without needing to have a 500-page presentation of the vision, mission, objectives and policies of the company for the next 10 years, stakeholders will want to hear that there is a credible future. Your job is not to come up with the answer on your own but to enable your team to develop and buy in to a compelling proposition. This is likely to require you to be both visionary and pace setting in your management style. People may need some strong leadership before they shake off deeply held existing views and assumptions which they will have to do in order to create a range of new possibilities for the business.

My experience is that after a crisis that has generated liquidity issues, the strategy formulation process is often driven by the perceived requirements of the financial stakeholders. This involves management working out how much profit and cash needs to be generated and then working back to the most achievable combination of sales volumes, prices, cost reductions, capital spending and disposals to achieve this. I would call this 'the pragmatic capitalist' approach to strategy after a crisis. It is probably the one most used by companies that have faced a financial crisis. The basic steps are:

1. Work out how much profit and cash you need to generate to satisfy your concerned financial stakeholders, typically lenders or investors.
2. Translate these bottom line requirements into a series of scenarios involving different combinations of sales, costs, cash and disposals.
3. Pick the scenario that seems to be the most achievable or least risky and present that as a strategy.
4. Plan to achieve the sales volumes, cost reductions and disposals to execute the strategy.

Some companies carry out what they consider to be a less cynical approach to strategy formulation. They add a first step by asking those in the business what they think the strategy and objectives should be. This output is then compared with step one above and the operating units are then told to deliver the results the financial stakeholders require. To me this is just the same process. I have often seen it done in non-crisis situations. Management teams work out what financial results are required to deliver the maximum incentive awards and work backwards to a strategy that could deliver those results.

I am not making any judgement on 'the pragmatic capitalist' approach to strategy development. The fact is that a lot of companies use it, although they might not be bold enough to admit internally, or externally, that is what they do. In addition, in a survival context, unless your plan is delivering what your key financial stakeholders consider is the minimum level of acceptable results, when they pull the plug you will fail all of your other stakeholders. The smart thing to do is to ensure that the translation of the financial objectives into customer promises, employee engagement and operating cost model is genuine. If you ride roughshod across the legitimate concerns of your operators, suppliers and customers you are likely to head for an even bigger crisis. In the Monty Python film *The Holy Grail* there was not enough money in the production budget to use real horses. Instead, the servants walked behind the knights and simulated the sound of horses by using coconut shells. This became one of the most entertaining parts of the film. So perhaps another name for this approach could also be 'necessity is the mother of invention'.

An alternative approach to the 'pragmatic capitalist' is the customer- or market-driven opportunity strategy. After a crisis you consider what the needs and requirements of different customer segments are and choose the opportunities that fit with the demands of your other stakeholders. As with the previous approach, a crisis often removes the luxury of free choice for management, which is why it is best to avoid one in the first place. Your strategy process might well identify a profitable and growing market segment that you could serve if you made a sizeable capital injection today. Unfortunately, the crisis that just hit the business has removed lenders' appetite to provide any new money.

A customer-led strategy process, combined with the constraints of the financial stakeholders, might, after a crisis, end up with some broad choices of direction:

- Cut back in order to grow. A period of asset disposal and shrinking the business in order to focus on a smaller, often geographic, customer segment which has medium-term growth potential.
- Get fit. The business is in good markets but has just not been competitive enough.
- Hold your breath. Reduce costs and improve cash flows without a drastic withdrawal from the customers and markets served, waiting until market growth returns.
- Save or dispose to invest. An opportunity for a valuable, growth-focused future exists but you need to generate the cash to invest from internal sources rather than external funds.
- Dress the bride. The impact of the crisis means that a medium-term independent future is not viable. The business needs to be prepared for sale with care in order to maximize value.

Generating these options and choosing the right one to follow is part of the leadership role you will need to play. Convincing others to support the choices you make, some of which might be very unpopular, is part of selling the recovery plan and is covered in Chapter 10.

Maintaining sales

It is an unfortunate fact of almost every business that sales revenue will always fall faster than you can cut costs. The financial dynamic of companies' profit and loss accounts is that the revenue line is much more variable than the costs lines. Even elements of your variable costs of goods sold, like raw materials, have to be bought some time in advance, tying up cash in working capital. This mismatch between the speed of a potential decline in demand and an ability to reduce costs correspondingly can turn a small problem into a full-blown liquidity crisis in just a short space of time.

From this it ought to be clear that maintaining sales during and after a crisis is one of the most important things to focus on. The nature of the crisis that has impacted the business will clearly steer the actions that need to be taken. Covering up a product defect for as long as possible to maintain sales is unlikely to be a smart thing to do. In fact, most of the case studies would suggest that the opposite is true. A total and rapid recall with substantive changes in production, quality and customer reassurance has proved to be a better strategy. The 1982 Tylenol poisoning episode, the detail of which is discussed by Stephen Greyser in a 1982 Harvard Business Review case study, provides a good example of rapid action and subsequent recovery in sales.

To assess the potential strategies for maintaining sales, I think there are three things you could start to think about.

First, the confidence of your sales people. After a crisis, in particular if it has been prominent in the media, your own employees' confidence will be depressed. In fact, in my view, the staff on the road meeting customers, in your call centres and retail stores will be more immediately affected than the executives in the boardroom. They will immediately face questions about the crisis and customers will get a sense of whether your staff are confident in the business and its products going forward and this feeling will influence a decision whether to make a purchase or not. It is, therefore, a priority to produce and communicate a set of 'questions and answers' for front line staff to use with customers. You may also add some extra tools for the sales staff to use to convince customers to carry on buying. After the initial impact of the credit crunch and subsequent recession in 2008/2009 a number of magazine and cable subscription companies allowed their sales agents to give, unpublicized, discounts to retain customers who were calling up to cancel.

The second area to look at in maintaining sales is your marketing and product development teams. Do these managers have the insights into how consumers and enterprises are reacting in harsher economic conditions or after a crisis? Drawing upon internal and external research and profiles, a house view could be quickly developed which summarizes both the historical models of how consumers and enterprises have reacted and future scenarios for how they might react. This could be used to inform thinking around:

- adapting the customer value propositions to reflect changing priorities and behaviours;
- brand thinking and new and existing product development investment cases;
- advertising priorities and channel changes;
- retention training and policies;
- credit terms and debt collection thinking;
- cost base reduction.

The important and urgent action is to communicate a shared view of the state of the customer's mind across the organization. This means that different departments are all using the same assumptions when interacting with customers to generate sales.

The third area to consider in maintaining sales after a crisis is the external messages you choose to communicate. When Tylenol was reintroduced into the market after the poisonings in 1982, it was accompanied by significant price reductions. Johnson & Johnson was keen to give customers an added reason to retry the product. After a crisis, you could consider adding, for a period of time, a feature, whether price, guarantee length, service in addition to the product's previous benefits. Just take care not to promise something that will have negative impacts worse than the potential lost sales. In 1992 the Hoover Company in the UK offered its customers free flights to the United States if they purchased more than £100 worth of their vacuum cleaners. Demand for the vacuum cleaners was huge and sales went up significantly. Unfortunately, the cost of the free flights was higher than the profit on the vacuum cleaners and the company ended up losing over £50 million.

Cost base restructuring

The flip side of striving to maintain sales income is to restructure the cost base to reflect the impact of the crisis and the proposed recovery strategy. Even outside of a crisis most companies are undertaking a constant series of cost reduction activities. If you look into the strategic priorities of some international fast moving consumer goods companies they can look very much alike, for example:

- Nestlé: 'innovation & renovation', 'operational efficiency', 'whenever, wherever, however', 'consumer communication';
- Colgate: 'succeeding with consumers, the profession and our customers', 'innovating everywhere', 'effectiveness and efficiency in everything', 'strengthening leadership worldwide';
- Carlsberg: 'step change innovation', 'commercial execution', 'efficiency', 'winning behaviours';
- Anheuser Busch InBev: 'connecting with customers', 'execution in the marketplace', 'financial and operational efficiency'.

The competitive advantage must come from something other than the building blocks of strategic intent, as these all seem quite similar. One of the pillars of each of these companies' operating model is a continuing reduction in costs. If this is delivered then any company which is not reducing costs to enable either better percentage margins or volume growth via price reductions, will be at a disadvantage. In fact this lack of competitiveness may have been a cause of the crisis that you are now facing. All of this makes how you approach setting the right cost base an important task. In the strategy section above, we identified some generic post-crisis strategies. Each of these provides a different context to the cost reduction tactics that you could employ:

- Cut back to grow. A sizeable part of the cost base will need to be reduced with many job losses and redundant assets to dispose of. However, an investment in the remaining core will be necessary.
- Get fit. The existing business may need to raise its net margins by 10, 20 or even 25 percentage points by increasing sales productivity and reducing the costs of operations and overheads.
- Hold your breath. Cost deferment and cost reduction need to be carried out to survive until the market returns, without permanently harming the business.
- Save or dispose to invest. Cost reduction efforts need to generate cash in the short to medium term, so the cash cost upfront of the cost restructuring cannot be too big.
- Dress the bride. Cost reductions can boost margins and therefore valuations but care has to be taken not to cut perceived marginal activities that a purchaser values.

This context can provide the backdrop to the type of interventions you make. A wide variety of cost reduction techniques exist to help you implement your chosen cost base restructuring strategy. These include:

- Business process reengineering. A management approach aimed at improving the efficiency and effectiveness of the processes that exist within and across organizations.
- Total Quality Management (TQM). Methods used to enhance quality and productivity. TQM is a system approach that works across an organization, involving all areas of the business, including suppliers and customers.
- Six Sigma. A rigorous approach to improving business processes by addressing the underlying causes of variation that lead to poor performance.
- Salami slicing. Refers to the arbitrary 'cut everything by 10 per cent' approach.
- Outsourcing. A practice used by companies to reduce costs, via focus and economies of scale, by transferring portions of work to outside suppliers.
- Offshoring. The relocation of business processes from one country to another. This includes any business process such as production, manufacturing or services. The economic logic is based on wage arbitrage, new technology capabilities and skilled resource.
- Activity-based costing (ABC). An accounting method to gather data about operating costs. Costs are assigned to specific activities such as planning, engineering, or manufacturing, and then the activities are associated with different products or services. In this way, the ABC method allows management to see which products and services are truly profitable and which are loss-making.
- Economies of scale. An increase in volume causes a decrease in the average cost of a unit or process.

Choosing the right approach will reflect the needs of the business and the capability of the organization. My experience is that the most popular cost reduction technique remains the salami slicing approach.

There is one other major area to consider in your cost reduction plans. A large part of many companies' cost base is the investment in new product development and launching new and revised products into markets. After a crisis, or in a recession, it may be that products that had been successful with customers before are no longer as relevant. If such changes to buying preferences have not been incorporated into the product development process quickly enough then a lot of cash could be wasted in launching products that will not sell.

As said before, it is an uncomfortable truth, but if you have just been through a crisis you are much more likely to suffer another in the next 12 months. This raises the question of cost reduction as a programme or as a way of life. For instance, Zero Based Budgeting (ZBB) is more like a methodology that becomes part of the fabric of a company rather than a discrete cost reduction programme. Every year, all existing costs are assumed to be reset to zero. All costs for the following year have to be justified, so there is none of the 'last year less 2 per cent' style of budgeting. The organization learns to operate in this type of way and there is no need for special cost requiring top-level sponsorship to succeed. One of the few commercial companies to make it work is the brewer, Anheuser-Busch InBev.

Core business skills

The four core skill areas outlined in this chapter and Chapter 7 can hopefully provide some thoughts about the business skills that may be helpful in planning and delivering your recovery plan. The final two chapters turn to the issues of making the plan come to life.

9 Delivering results through relationships

When I worked as a partner in a restructuring practice in the late 1990s, we were asked by colleagues in corporate finance to take on a new director from the mergers and acquisitions part of the business and who did not seem to be fitting in there. This man had excellent technical skills and was well liked by staff but his inability to relate to clients appeared to be a weakness. He was considered blunt and insensitive to the political aspects of building good business relationships. Our colleagues in corporate finance thought the restructuring practice would be an ideal place for him to work because it did not require the same level of relationship skills as M&A did. Their assumption was that helping companies after a crisis was all about blunt management and highly directive leadership. Raised voices, sharp elbows and a just do it attitude were surely the only people skills necessary. We politely declined the offer of the transfer.

A turnaround, restructuring or crisis situation certainly does require decisive management, clear direction setting and an ability to perform under intense pressure. But the most successful restructuring leaders I have worked with have also had outstanding relationship skills. They listen well, seek out a variety of opinions and set clear visions in highly uncertain circumstances. Most importantly, they understand that to develop and deliver a recovery plan they are going to have to ask a disparate set of stakeholders to commit to the necessary changes. I would argue that leading a recovery is one of the toughest tests to which you can put your leadership and relationship management skills.

I said right back at the start of this book, there comes a point in your management career when you will no longer be able to deliver results just through your own personal efforts. The CEO of a mining company cannot hit production targets by putting in overtime on the digger trucks. You have to be able to deliver results through other people and at the very heights of leadership you have to deliver them through a number of layers of management to reach the front line workers. This ability is a cornerstone of all forms of leadership. In fact, I always prefer the definition of 'leadership' as 'followership' – you have to persuade people to choose to follow you. To illustrate the point, I drew the following diagram (Figure 9.1) for a global telecommunications firm.

The cloud at the top was their 200 million customers worldwide. The inverted pyramid was the 50,000 employees in the business with, near its point, the 200 strong senior management team and the executive committee of 15 people and, at the very apex, the CEO. The CEO and the executive committee had to be able to engage the senior managers, middle managers, team leaders and, eventually, the front line employees in the call centres and stores to engage and interact with the 200 million customers in a way that produced the desired results.

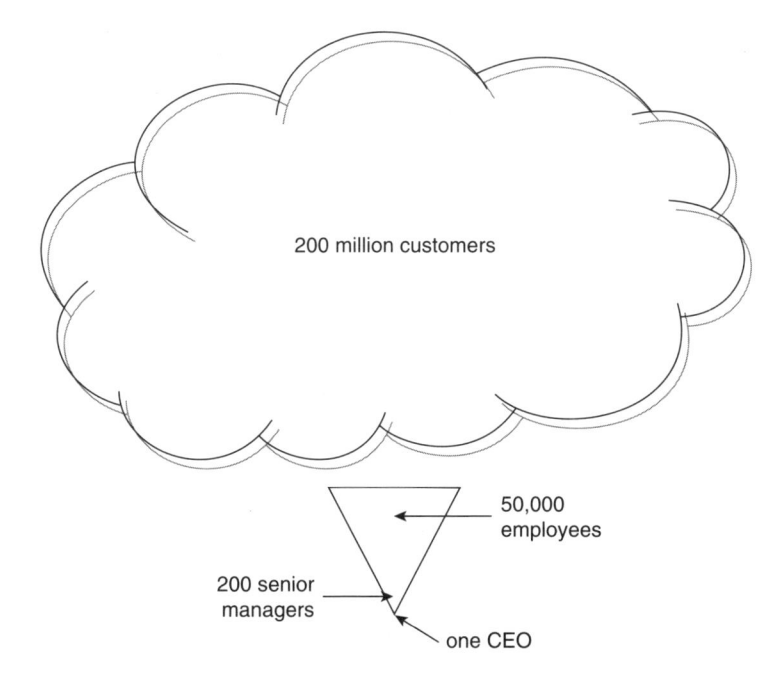

Figure 9.1 Delivering results through others

Over the years I have worked in partnership with the international leadership consultancy, Hay Group, on a number of clients. They, together with their McClelland research centre, first introduced me to the idea of 'discretionary effort'. The basic idea is that every day when each of us turns up for work we keep a certain amount of discretionary effort tucked into our pockets. Depending on how we feel about our job, the people we work with and the leaders around us we choose to deploy all, some or none of it that day. The more of that discretionary effort a leader can persuade an employee to release, the better the results for the company. Being able to tap into this additional discretionary effort from multiple stakeholders, including employees, is critical to the success of any recovery from a crisis.

In this chapter, I want to share with you one tool that, coming from my experience working on recovery plan implementations, I have found to be of help in releasing that discretionary effort. It is summarized in Figure 9.2 below.

```
         ┌─────────┐
         │ Results │
       ┌─┴─────────┴─┐
       │   Actions   │
     ┌─┴─────────────┴─┐
     │ Operating model │
   ┌─┴─────────────────┴─┐
   │    Possibilities    │
 ┌─┴─────────────────────┴─┐
 │      Relationships      │
 └─────────────────────────┘
```

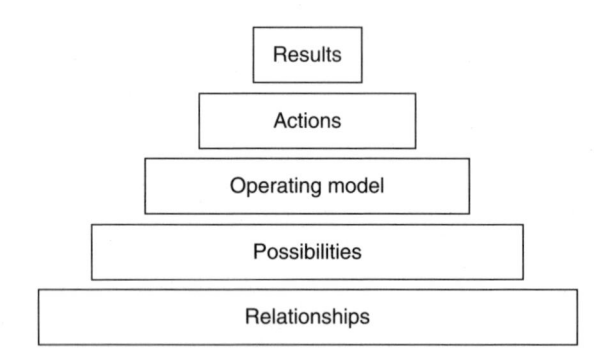

Figure 9.2 Relationships to results pyramid

I mentioned this tool first in Chapter 1, remarking that it provides a framework for considering how strategy is translated into results, without actually using the word 'strategy'. It is a way to focus leadership activity on the actions that will make a real difference to delivering results. I have searched for the original source of the model but been unable to find it in any literature, so I apologize to whoever did the initial work for not being able to credit you here.

The basic proposition is this. As a leader following a crisis where do you spend your time most effectively? At the sharp end of the crisis? Directing actions? You will also have to consider strategy and operations. You will need to lead a process of thinking about new opportunities for the business. A critical role for you will be to manage the expectations of different and possibly conflicting stakeholders. But you cannot do everything yourself. Once you accept this, then you have to find a way to deliver results through other people. What are the things that you can do to enable other people to be more capable and more motivated? How do you spend your long working day effectively delivering the recovery plan through inspiring others to do the right things?

I hope that by exposing you to this model you may gain some insights that help you be more capable in this area of leadership.

Overview

I will remind you that the theory behind this approach is based on the proposition that business results can only be achieved by taking actions and the actions taken determine the results achieved. This is the essence of the 'just do it' approach and has complete validity. If you do nothing, nothing will happen. Right? Well, maybe not. If you do nothing, lots of things will still happen but they may not be the things you want to happen. An absence of positive action will cause stakeholders to make their own decisions since they will see a vacuum of leadership from you. Doing nothing may, of course, be the result of a conscious, pragmatic and, in some circumstances, correct decision.

If you want to deliver results, people have to take some sort of action. The question is what? Two things influence those actions: the results you are asking people to achieve and the operating model that guides which actions people choose to take. When I was at University, in vacations I worked at an electrical goods store. We sold televisions, hi-fi and video equipment. The store management had always used an individual commission system for rewarding sales staff like me. The basic hourly pay was very small but you could earn a good wage by selling high volumes of product on commission. This 'operating model' encouraged a certain type of behaviour and consequent actions. Those sales staff like me, hungry because they had student loans to pay, fought tooth and nail for every customer. We would sell anything and everything to a customer, whether needed or not. The results were good for the business but the atmosphere amongst the staff was highly competitive and actually detrimental to customer service. The store had a reputation for great deals but also for high pressure sales tactics. The actions that we took as sales staff were a reflection of the operating model that the management had chosen to put in place. The results were good short-term sales figures at the expense of a longer-term brand perception from customers.

At some point management thought up a new approach. If the commission system was changed to be on a team basis then there would be less aggressive individual behaviour and better customer satisfaction. A new results and rewards system was put in place and a new operating model established. The actions sales staff took changed as a result. And, as actions determine results, the outcomes also changed as a consequence of the change in targets and operating model. Now in many businesses I worked with later such a change in targets and operating model produced actions that delivered the results the leadership team sought. In this case, though, the results were awful. Why should I work that hard to sell to customers just to have to share the commission with the laziest member of the team? Before the change there would be a race to speak to a customer first and start the sales process. Now, most of the sales staff stood around waiting for a customer to speak to them. Sales and motivation both went down as a result. I put forward this example not to suggest that individual commission is the right way to manage sales staff but, rather, that what happens by way of results reflects the targets and operating model a leader puts in place.

This takes us back to our model. As a leader, it is critical you have the right targets and operating model in place. So the next question is where you go to find the right targets and operating model to ensure employees act in the way you want.

The next layer under the operating model in our pyramid is possibilities. In Chapter 6 we talked about taking a 360 degree view of your business and market to identify new ideas and opportunities. In a recovery plan we discussed how important it was to seek out different perspectives to construct and implement a successful restructuring. Those new possibilities could open the door to different operating models, strategies and ambitions. The 'just do it' method would focus on taking action now. Important as this is during a stabilization period it could blinker you to a more value-creating future. And in Chapter 6, we saw the source of new possibilities was listening to a wider audience of views.

This takes us down to the foundation of the pyramid model. The source of new ideas, better operating models, improved actions and the results you want is the relationships that you build inside and outside the business. The better those relationships are, the better business results you will deliver.

What does better relationships mean? Obviously, not that you are friends with more people. There is both a quantity and quality element. I have referred a number of times before to the leadership 'wobble board' (see Figure 9.3).

You will remember the wobble board represents the challenge to management and leadership of balancing the competing demands of different stakeholders – investors and lenders, customers, employees and suppliers, and could include regulators or government. The point is that there are a range of people you will need to build relationships with in order to

```
                    Customers
                       and
                    Consumers
                        ↑
                        |
  Investors          ┌──────┐
    and      ←───────│Business│───────→  Suppliers
   Lenders          │ Leader │
                    └──────┘
                        |
                        ↓
                    Employees
```

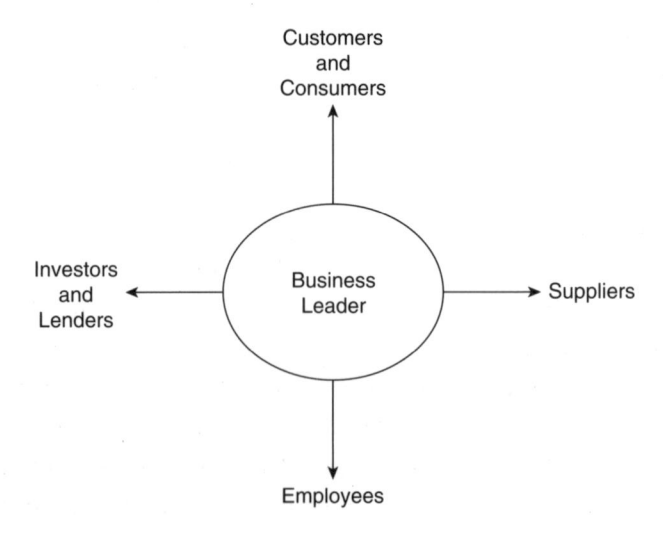

Figure 9.3 Leadership wobble board

build and execute your recovery plan. It is not sufficient to rely on a narrow range of relationships where you feel comfortable. One restructuring after a crisis that I advised on in 2009, for a US/European industrial group, required the leadership team to build relationships with the following stakeholders:

- a syndicate of 12 lending banks;
- nine mezzanine finance providers;
- two credit insurance companies;
- two credit rating agencies;
- a bonding line provider;
- two sets of lawyers;
- government customers in 22 countries;
- 30 senior managers and 800 employees;
- pension regulators;
- competition authorities;
- a private equity house;
- three trade unions;
- trade press journalists;

- two consulting firms;
- at least 30 key suppliers.

All of these people had a greater or lesser role to play in bringing about a successful recovery plan. Each of them was important in creating new opportunities and possibilities for the business and establishing a new operating model. All of them had to take actions that contributed to the results we were seeking. As a business leader, your role is to act as the ringmaster, knowing everybody and having a sufficient relationship with them to gain their trust and contribution.

This brings into focus what the quality of the relationship needs to be. Clearly it will be different for different stakeholders. For your top team a quality relationship means that the team members are releasing their maximum discretionary efforts to achieve the plan. It can be measured by the contribution they are making to developing and accepting the changes that will be needed. It can also be measured by the success that the team has in selling the plan to the rest of the business.

We can now look at each aspect of the model individually.

Results

After a crisis it will be necessary in the short term to set clear targets for individuals and the business. My experience is that a wholesale and immediate change in targets and objectives can be more unsettling than the crisis itself. After a crisis, people are faced with increased uncertainty about the business and any impact it may have had on them personally. One strategy for the very short term is to ask people, especially employees, to continue to focus on 'business as usual'. If you choose to do this you should at the same time communicate a clear timetable of when they will be updated on what is happening and stick to that communication plan. The one area of certainty you can bring to the situation is a timetable of consultations and updates. A small piece of certainty perhaps but at least that way people know when they will hear further information. At the same time, with a smaller group of senior managers, you can start to develop the content for that communication and plan the first steps of the recovery plan.

What results should you be planning for? This is clearly dependent on the circumstances of the business and what needs to be done to gain the time and support of the most relevant stakeholders. There is not much point in undertaking extensive new consumer research if you do not have enough cash to make payroll at the end of the month. In another situation consumer engagement was the most critical aspect of building a recovery plan. For example, the new CEO of a supermarket ended up setting a few critical targets for the business:

- deliver sales growth of $3 billion over four years;
- achieve operating cost savings of $500 million within two years;
- deliver a $500 million catch up price investment to customers;
- invest 1% to 1.5% in price cuts annually.

The targets he set illustrate two points for us. First, the targets fed into a thought-through recovery plan for the business that made sense for a mass market supermarket retailer. Let's just look at the economics of a single store using the $100 model we discussed in Chapter 6. A significant proportion of a store's costs are in effect fixed, such as rent and rates on the building, depreciation for the costs of fitting out the store, the IT system and even the infrastructure costs of the supply chain. The staff costs are also broadly fixed, given levels of service standards and opening hours. So the economics mean that with a contribution after the costs of goods sold in the region of 15 to 20 per cent, additional sales are going to flow straight through to bottom line profitability. Any additional sales that contribute after the fixed costs are covered provide an outstanding return. Pretty obvious, you say, but how do mass market supermarkets generate extra sales? In this particular case the supermarket had lost its way in actual and perceived price competitiveness. As the core strategy of one of its rivals spelled out, 'We sell more volume, to grow bigger, to get cheaper, to sell more volume, to grow bigger,' etc, etc.

In order to price its products more cheaply the business had to save money in other areas. The cost reduction target matched the investment in product price reductions. Then, every year they needed to find the savings to reduce prices further for customers by 1 to 1.5 per cent, which would drive the sales target growth of $3 billion. To me, this was a clear, well thought through set of targets. They were simple to explain and made sense to just about everybody both inside and outside of the business. The lesson could be that the targets that you set for the first and later stages of your recovery plan need to be few in number and make common business sense. Also, your targets could need to change over the period of the plan. Timely setting of a small number of targets for the here and now could be better than letting time elapse while you consider a set of targets that make sense over a two- or three-year period.

One last point on results. They must be capable of being monitored in a timely and relevant way. In addition, you need to monitor the probability of achieving future targets and not just report on the historic results.

Actions

The next layer of the model is about the actions that are being taken. As discussed, it is the actions that employees and other stakeholders take that actually determine results. At a very basic level there can be a state of corporate paralysis after a crisis that results in no one doing anything very differently. People become too afraid to take risks and the classic delaying processes of asking for more data and more analysis take over from real decision making. Your role is to ensure that people at all levels have sufficient guidance and confidence to make decisions and not to try to make every decision yourself. We shall look at two contrasting approaches to helping employees make better decisions and take the right actions.

Remember that in Chapter 4 we talked about the failure of a home delivery kitchen business. The flip side of this failure was the success of the trade supply kitchen business which was also part of the same group. The operating model for this business was to supply local tradesmen, builders and kitchen fitters, with all of the product and services they needed to sell and install kitchens in their local area. The founder of the business had the insight to understand that most local kitchen fitters were always short of cash and time. He therefore built a business that was absolutely focused on making more money for the local fitters and their jobs easier. The original operating model design and any major changes to it were the sole responsibility of the founding CEO and reflected his style of leadership. But he recognized he could not be in the room every time a decision was being made or an action taken in any one of the hundreds of depots that the business operated. How could he influence each of the local managers and employees to take the right actions? What he developed was a purpose statement for the business that brought together the core business elements of the operating model. The original statement was that the purpose of the business was to 'Supply the routine kitchen and joinery needs of builders from local stock, with no call back quality, at best local price'.

No matter what the type of stakeholder, he would start every meeting he had with this statement and by doing so taught the organization how to use it in their day-to-day operations. The statement itself contains several internal conflicts. How do you achieve at the same time the best local price and no call back quality? How do you stock all the routine needs of the builder and always be in stock? What is 'routine' anyway? Paradoxically, the internal conflicts actually help managers and staff have a valuable debate about the decisions they take. It is almost like having the founding CEO in the room with you. Two very important reasons why this business approach was successful were that the statement made good, common business sense and the core of the message has remained unchanged for 15 years.

In the world of international companies, too, you will find examples of how leaders have sought to guide the actions of employees through the use of purpose statements. The pharmaceutical company Johnson & Johnson has a credo that explains the philosophy and work practices of the business.

Does your company have an official or unofficial purpose statement that people understand and use in their day-to-day decision making? If not, what context do they use to make decisions and take actions? Incentive schemes, local rules and policies or gut feel? After a crisis, when uncertainty has increased, it can be exceptionally valuable to have an authentic purpose and context for people to rely on. I have asked many executives at numerous companies if they can write a statement for their business similar to the trade kitchen supply business. It is surprising and disappointing how many of the attempts fail to meet a standard that would be helpful for guiding action within their business.

The second approach that we can look at in relation to the actions that generate results is standard operating procedures ('SOPs'). Each SOP is a clear, documented way to undertake a task to produce a result. It has developed from the military through to an essential part of total quality systems and lean management techniques. For our purposes there is one aspect of SOPs I want to focus on – how they help your employees closest to the coalface of the business drive productivity improvements. A good SOP is a result of the accumulated knowledge of the many people involved in designing and operating a process over the years. In an automobile factory, for example, there will be an SOP for each particular part of a process to assemble and check each car produced. The SOPs allow routine tasks to be performed efficiently, with high quality and by different employees. It was told to me on a visit to Toyota City in Japan that each employee of Toyota had two responsibilities. Apply the standard as set and look for ways to improve it. The presence of a clear, documented way of undertaking a task actually allows a worker the freedom to consider how to improve it. 'Standardizing' the work had the reverse impact to making the job boring. It allowed people the time and freedom to be more innovative. In contrast, a business without SOPs can spend most of its time and intellectual effort fighting fires and producing workarounds. The perceived freedom to act actually drains employees of a lot of their discretionary effort and there is less time to think about how to improve the business and to innovate.

Operating model

This last thought brings us to the third layer. The operating model includes the organizational structure of the business, the skill and motivation of the people in relevant roles, performance management and incentivization, processes and IT systems and leadership and people development. It also includes the decision about whether to use a particular management approach such as SOPs, Six Sigma, lean thinking or open innovation. This is the heart, soul and engine room of the business and determines the actions and decisions that are taken by the business on a day-to-day basis. The top team has the responsibility for the overall design and updating of the operating model to reflect market developments and changing opportunities. The right design for the operating model should be inspired by the quality and range of possibilities that are open to the business. These include which customers and markets to serve, the range and type of products and services to offer and developments in, for example, IT, that affect how products and services can be delivered.

After a crisis it will probably be necessary to do two things in parallel. In the short term you will need to ensure that the existing operating model can continue to function and deliver sales, profits and, most importantly, cash. You may have to make some changes to it, particularly if it was a failure of the operating model that caused the crisis. Secondly, you will need to start to develop a model that is appropriate to the post-crisis situation you must now operate within. The role of the leadership team is to ensure that the right number and quality of new possibilities are being generated and that legacy opportunities that are no longer viable do not preclude development of the right operating model.

One approach to developing a new operating model after a crisis is to use one of the many customer-led management design techniques. Lean thinking is one of these tools but because of its name it has often been misused by companies large and small. True lean thinking is a highly customer-focused philosophy with a large number of management tools and processes associated with it. It is a pity that many management teams become obsessed with the tools – Kanban, Andon boards, Kaizen, 5S and the rest – at the expense of the core customer thinking. For me, at the very core of the lean thinking philosophy are some choices that have to be made:

- Which customers is it possible for me to serve now and in the future?
- Of these, which customers will I choose to serve?
- What are the fundamental needs of those customer groups?
- What do I need to do to serve those fundamental needs?
- Can I align my business around those fundamental needs and eliminate any other activity that does not serve those fundamental needs and is therefore waste, or *'muda'*?
- Can momentum in the business be driven by customer demand rather than management push?
- If so, can I arrange the flow of my business to meet actual customer requests?
- Does this operating model make a cash return profit?
- Is there something in it for all stakeholders – investors and lenders, customers, employees and suppliers?

This type of thinking has resulted in the many low cost business models that have replaced the more traditional operators as leaders in the fields of air travel, hotels, car insurance and banking.

Whatever approach you use to determine a refreshed operating model for the business after a crisis, the results will only be as good as the ideas and energy that go into the process, which we will consider below.

Possibilities and relationships

The inputs into the development of your operating model and the resultant actions and results are driven by the range and quality of possibilities that you consider. The better the ideas and thinking, the better the results. The proposition is that it is the relationships that exist within a business and between a business, its customers, suppliers and other stakeholders that drive innovation and new opportunities. Therefore, the role of the leader after a crisis is to ensure that within the business the right quality and scope of relationships are being established.

In the final chapter we will discuss the last of the five areas of expertise to help you lead after a crisis. This is about building or rebuilding trust with key stakeholders through authentic communication and is the essential part of establishing stronger and better quality relationships.

Before that we should consider how you split your time between the different elements of the model. The answer here depends on the situation you are facing and you should be sensitive to the needs of the business and its stakeholders in how and where you spend your time. I have characterized below the extremes of some of the leadership approaches I have seen after a crisis.

We have the 'Big Picture Person'. Despite the fact that the business has gone through a major crisis the leader is still acting as if the day-to-day detail of the business is not an essential part of finding a solution. This leadership style tends to focus on strategy, corporate M&A possibilities and grand designs. Leaders will spend their time with advisors rather than their own staff and can focus too much on share prices and financial stakeholders. Middle managers, in the midst of fighting a major operational crisis, sit in meetings with such leaders wondering what planet they are from.

Next, we have the 'Red Adair', the 'lead from the front' style of leader who feels most comfortable in the trenches with the front line employees, sorting out the crisis one fire at a time. This leader often has an excellent understanding and empathy for the business and strong relationships with a small number of people. He or she does not spend a lot of time on new possibilities and developing wider relationships and sometimes finds it hard to understand why it is necessary to spend any time at all with investors or bankers. Red Adair also has an intense dislike of consultants.

Finally, we have the 'Silk Suit'. This leadership style reflects a belief that success is solely about relationships. Such leaders spend almost all their time building new relationships across a variety of stakeholders, often including the media and politicians, and they tend to sit on the most prestigious charity committees. Surprisingly, they can often be seen at the coalface of the business with staff and customers but unlike the Red Adair leader they may not want to get blood on their suits. Silk suits can often switch jobs between companies.

The point of these caricatures is to make you think about how and where you spend your time – do you look anything like any of these three stereotypical leaders? The most important thing, I believe, is you understand where your own leadership preferences are and can be flexible in how you respond to the challenges of a crisis.

10 Rebuilding trust with authentic communication

Before we start this last chapter perhaps we should review what we have already covered and draw a few conclusions.

Chapters 2, 3 and 4 defined what a crisis is and examined some of the internal and external causes of a crisis. A key message was that one of the main triggers for a business crisis is when stakeholders change assumptions about the future of a company. Such assumptions might be about sales growth rates, profitability, ability to pay suppliers or product safety. In Chapter 5 we considered a roadmap for where to start in building your recovery plan and the first area of leadership expertise – making the right promises. After that we looked at three further areas of leadership expertise you could develop in order to manage more effectively after a crisis.

A few themes have been present through all of the preceding chapters:

- Too narrow a set of perspectives or viewpoints on your business and market can be a cause of a crisis and inhibit the building of a credible recovery plan.
- To understand the problems and develop possible solutions you will have to spend time at the coalface of the business.
- Assumptions are dangerous. Treat the assumptions you make about the future with great care.
- Promises to stakeholders need to be balanced, as each stakeholder must have a reason to support the recovery plan.

Relevant to all of these themes, especially the development of valuable relationships, is the building of trust inside and outside of your company. It is this issue of trust and how to re-establish it that is the focus of the last area of leadership expertise and of this final chapter.

After a crisis, trust levels between the company, its customers, employees, suppliers and financial stakeholders can be at dangerously low levels. This lack of trust can lead to cash and time problems, missing out on opportunities when an upturn happens and, very often, a change of management. In earlier chapters we talked about the various ways that stakeholders lose confidence in a business and its managers. One of them was when management broke promises made to a stakeholder. In attempting to understand trust in a business context we need to have some definition of what we mean. Although trust is a word overused in business it, nevertheless, does not have a clear, shared definition amongst most business people. If the term can mean different things it can be doubly challenging for a team tasked with 'rebuilding trust' to know what to do.

I introduced the tool that we use to develop expertise in this area in Chapter 1. It is based on a very practical approach to defining and rebuilding trust. As I said, I am indebted to the work of David Maister *et al* (2000), in their book *The Trusted Advisor*, although in this case I am using a version adapted by business consultant and advisor, Yuda Tuval (see Figure 10.1).

$$\text{Trust} = \frac{(\text{Benefit} - \text{Cost}) \times \text{Intimacy}}{\text{Perceived Risk}}$$

Figure 10.1 Trust equation

The equation is a framework for us to think about trust and how to rebuild it after a crisis. To start with, we can define each element of the trust equation in the context of leading after a crisis.

Trust

The first challenge is to define how we would measure business trust. Can you define and measure trust in the same way as you would sales, cash or profits? Unfortunately, there is no international accounting standard for trust. To bring a practical element to this and to try to bring the measurement of trust to life for managers, I use a stakeholder analysis table similar to that developed and used by many consulting firms (see Figure 10.2).

Stakeholder	Stop	Negative	Positive	Make	Lead
Lender ABC		C	R		
Customer Acme			CR		
Supplier 123	C			R	
CFO			C		R
Supply chain director				CR	
Store staff			C	R	

Figure 10.2 Stakeholder analysis table

You should construct four separate tables for each of the stakeholders that we described as forming the leadership 'wobble board' – investors and lenders, customers, employees and suppliers – and they should show each of the key stakeholders in the first column and the critical individuals within each of them. The next five columns show where each stakeholder and individual might stand in relation to the recovery plan:

- Stop it happening. This stakeholder, or these individuals, have such a low level of trust in the management and/or recovery plan that they will actively seek to stop the plan being implemented.
- Negative support. While not actively trying to stop the recovery plan, there is not enough interest or trust in it for the stakeholder to do anything helpful. If the stakeholder were forced to make a decision it would likely be negative.
- Positive support. This stakeholder has sufficient interest and trust to play a passive, but supportive role in the recovery plan. However, your plan is not an essential part of their own priorities.
- Make it happen. This stakeholder or individual will take proactive, positive steps to make the recovery plan successful.
- Lead the plan. These are the small number of people and stakeholders who will drive the process of recovery after a crisis.

For each stakeholder and individual you and your management team need to take a view as to where they currently sit. Mark this with a 'C' in the appropriate column. In plotting where people currently are, take a conservative and realistic stance. The next step is to plot where you require an individual or institution to be for this phase of the recovery plan to be successful by marking an 'R' in the appropriate column. You may need various versions of these tables to cover the short-, medium- and long-term phases of your recovery plan.

The final step is to stand back and consider what the table is telling you and your team. Where the C and the R are in the same column for a stakeholder then you are in the happy position of already having the required level of trust that you need from that person to deliver the recovery plan. The risk you must manage is of destroying trust with that stakeholder, for example by broken promises in the recovery phase, and of the C rating moving to the left of the R. Even better, there may be some stakeholders with a current position to the right of the required position. Where this is the case you ought to ask why. Has the person misunderstood what the situation is and what might be required of them? Perhaps they have another reason for demonstrating such apparent, unsolicited support. Or maybe they are just a very well-motivated stakeholder.

In the early stages the current position of a stakeholder is usually to the left of where you require them to be. People do not yet have enough trust in you, your team or the recovery plan. This is the gap that we are seeking to close. There are two ways you can fill it. Either reduce your planned reliance on that stakeholder, in effect moving the R to the left, or increase the level of trust that the person has and move the C to the right. To close the gap by increasing trust you will have to be effective in the content of what you are doing and in the way you communicate actions and results to that stakeholder. The previous chapters of this book have covered many of the content issues that you will have to consider in determining your plan. This chapter looks at how you can be effective in communicating that content.

Once you have established these tables you can use them as part of your planning and monitoring process for the duration of the recovery plan. Considering how each stakeholder moves to the left and right should give you some insights into the trajectory of your results.

Benefits less costs = value

The first part of the trust equation is about the tangible business value that you are bringing to a stakeholder as a result of the implementation of the recovery plan. Or, to put it more simply, what is in it for me, the stakeholder? If the business benefits from the plan are inconsequential for a person or institution why should they bother to support it? Worse still, if a stakeholder has assumed they would be reaping significant benefits from the plan and then discover they are not, they are only human; they may take action to thwart your proposals.

I like to think of the challenge of communicating value to stakeholders as an advertising campaign. An advert has a very short amount of time to convince a potential customer there is value for them in the product offering. Let us take two extremes of advertising as potential examples: a mass market carpet retailer and a luxury watchmaker.

The carpet retailer has an advert board outside every store with the caption, 'There is one outstanding reason to visit us – we are cheaper than everybody else'. This is a clear statement of value. If the quality of our carpets is sufficient for your needs, the basic benefit to you, then the value of that benefit will be higher because the costs to you will be less than if you buy the same carpet from anybody else. The simple equivalent in a recovery plan would be a financial return promise. Invest money in our turnaround and we will provide you with a valuable return on that investment.

But the benefits people look for are not all financial. Some stakeholders will be interested in the benefits, or damage, to their reputations, personal pride, sense of responsibility and position in society. The costs to them of their time and inconvenience may figure as greatly as any return of cash and profits. The second extreme of adverts illustrates this. See if you can find on Google Images the Patek Philippe advert showing a father and son sitting together, with the caption 'You never actually own a Patek Philippe. You merely look after it for the next generation'. A Patek Philippe watch can cost tens of thousands of dollars to own. If you only wanted a watch to tell the time then buying a Patek Philippe would be a very poor bargain. So the advert does not tell you about the benefits of the watch's time keeping capabilities; it persuades you to feel less guilty about buying a beautiful watch for yourself today, because one day you will hand it on to your son as an heirloom.

When a stakeholder is asked by their boss about why they are supporting your recovery plan they will need to have a rational, business-focused reason to give. The answer will need to be concise, thought through and credible. If, as a stakeholder, it is difficult to frame an answer to the question of why they are supporting the plan then they are less likely to support it. If you have not helped a stakeholder to be able to answer this question when you are not in the room, then you are putting your recovery plan at risk. Individual stakeholders will not be spending as much time and effort on your recovery plan as you are. The leadership team should be in the ideal position to help individual stakeholders to craft a response to questions about the crisis and the turnaround. To achieve this, you need to be able to stand in the shoes of different stakeholders and see the world from their standpoints. You need to be able to prepare questions and credible answers from each stakeholder's point of view. I am still amazed by the split of time that leadership teams place on their formal PowerPoint presentation compared with preparing the Q&As. Normal communication between people does not happen via a slide show. Slide shows are not communication as defined as a two-way dialogue. Think about the conversations you have with people every day:

> 'How are you?'
> 'What did you think of the game?'

'Who do you think will succeed the marketing director?'
'Where is the next sales conference being held?'

When creating your communications to rebuild trust, they need to be 'authentic'. One aspect of being authentic is that the communication happens in a way that reflects real human interaction. At the risk of committing heresy I do not consider communication by PowerPoint and bullet point lists to be authentic. In fact, sometimes they can be a substitute for clear thinking.

If PowerPoint is not an authentic communication tool, what is? My suggestion is that stories and Q&A are a good place to start. Stories that illustrate your point, provide a challenging or alternative perspective and are easy to remember can have a much more powerful impact on people. They also require less set-up and can happen spontaneously in the boardroom, corridor or factory floor without the need of a laptop, screen or projector. The Q&A provide the responses to the questions people have about your recovery story.

Another tool you might consider in preparing your communication around the rational value of your plan is set out in Figure 10.3 below.

Feel	Think
Say	Do

Figure 10.3 Communication planning grid

Before committing pen to paper ahead of a communication, spend some time thinking what impact you would like to have. From the perspective of the audience, how would you like them to feel and think? And what do you want them to say and do at the end of your presentation?

Intimacy

The next part of the trust equation is about the quality and quantity of your interactions with each stakeholder. You may have developed a revolutionary recovery plan that will change the face of the commercial world but if nobody knows who you are, their trust in you will be zero. Anything big multiplied by zero is still zero. The questions to ask yourself are:

- How much business intimacy do I need with each stakeholder to move the trust level so the C and the R are in the same column?
- What forms of communication are open to me to build intimacy?
- How much time do I need to devote to deliver the communication?

As with the analogy we used earlier about adverts, you can think about your communication plans as a 'campaign'. In his books and lectures about strategy and leadership the London Business School Professor Costas Markides refers to the critical need for managers to 'sell' ideas to their people. I suggest that you think about your recovery plan as an advertising campaign that needs to be sold. One of the companies that has used the concept of business intimacy as a core business message is UBS Wealth Management. Their 'You & Us' campaign included powerful photographs showing just two people in conversation. It is not clear which is the client and which is the banker. What is clear from the photographs is that they have a close, trusting business partnership. There is a high level of business intimacy.

The amount of intimacy required and the form of communication will be closely linked. On a scale of intimacy building potential I would rank some of the available options in the following order, with the most intimate first.

1. one-to-one, face-to-face meeting;
2. a few-to-one, face-to-face meeting;
3. a few-to-few, face-to-face meeting;
4. as above but via telephone;
5. as above but via videoconference / webinar;
6. unplanned, soap box meeting with a team;
7. Town Hall meeting with the team;
8. personal, handwritten letter;
9. personal, typed letter;
10. personal e-mail;
11. set piece presentations;
12. video e-mail to many;
13. e-mail announcements to many.

Whatever your personal view of the rankings, I would argue that the extremes of the scale are a one-to-one meeting in person and mass e-mail announcements. Clearly, the extremes also involve the opposite in terms of time commitment. Holding one-to-ones with 10,000 employees is difficult. Sending them an e-mail is time-efficient.

The point is that if the only communication you use has a low intimacy quotient then the message content itself had better be very convincing of the benefits and costs of the recovery plan. The weaker or more complex the value of your arguments the more intimate the nature of your communication will need to be. Clearly, the answer is to build a campaign that uses all the relevant forms of communication to produce a blend of efficiency and intimacy.

The advent of social networking and the internet has reinforced the effectiveness of viral marketing. However, even before technology made the spread of messages quicker and more widespread, there has always been viral marketing – it was just called word of mouth. The important aspect of a good viral marketing campaign is that the story to be spread is both interesting and easy to pass on. For your recovery plan to be successful you need an interesting story about it that is easy to pass on. Look at the long-running Avis car rental slogan of 'We try harder'. All companies have their own collection of myths, stories and beliefs. As part of your recovery communication plan see if you can create an authentic tag line or story that will resonate with your people.

Perceived risk

The last part of the trust equation focuses on the risks that the stakeholders see in committing their time, money, credibility and discretionary effort to the recovery plan. Note that this is not your view of the actual risks they face but the stakeholders' own perception of the risks. As I have said many times before in these pages, to be successful in this area will require you to be able to stand in the shoes of your stakeholders and genuinely understand their point of view. This, to me, is one of the key components of what I mean by being authentic. You make a genuine effort to understand the other person's point of view. The other key aspects of authenticity are that you do not try to be somebody you are not and you do not try to cover up the problems your business is facing. A quickly made, sincere apology and acceptance of responsibility can go a long way to re-establishing a base to build trust after a crisis. Denial, a vacuum of communication, or weasel words could just reinforce stakeholders' negative views about your management.

So what are the perceived risks that stakeholders could have about your recovery plan? Clearly the greater they see those risks to be, the lower the level of trust they have that you can deal with them.

For employees, the perceived risks could be associated with their own job security, pension entitlements, career progression or standing within the company. If your recovery plan is the fourth one in five years then employees are likely to be sceptical about any new plans from the leadership team. If your company has an internal reputation of saying one thing but the leadership doing another, then the risks employees perceive is going to be high. As uncertainty will already be high after a crisis, so perceived risk is likely to be even higher. On the other hand, I have often found that many managers and front line staff were well aware of the impending crisis before it happened. An authentic acknowledgement of the previous problems and a willingness to address the real issues can be warmly welcomed by employees.

Customers will also have their own set of perceived risks about your business. Is it safe to continue to trade with this business? Will they be around to service my purchase in the years to come? How will buying from a company after a crisis look to my boss? Could I be criticized for continuing to do business with this company? The old adage of never being criticized for buying IBM still applies to many situations after a crisis. Your communication message will need to focus on providing answers that customers can reassure themselves with about their future purchasing decisions.

For investors and lenders the perceived risks are likely to be both institutional and personal. On a corporate basis the financial stakeholders will need to decide on what terms, if at all, they continue to support the business. This is likely to boil down to whether they will enjoy a better financial return from the recovery plan or any other alternative options they have. On a personal basis, individuals will be concerned about the personal risks they run inside their own organizations by supporting the plan. How much personal risk do you need to ask people at your bank to take to recommend fresh lending to your business after a crisis?

Suppliers' primary concerns will be over whether they will be paid and if doing business with you in the future will enhance or damage their reputations. Their perceptions of the risk will be largely driven by what you are asking of them and their previous experience of your company. If your business has a reputation for nit-picking over invoices, 'cheques lost in the post' and delayed payment to creditors then you should expect a high level of perceived risk.

Trust and communication

The objective of the trust equation is to help you think about how you bring key stakeholders on side to support your recovery plan. Even if the quality of your plan and ideas are outstanding, a low level of acceptance by stakeholders means your results will be below requirement.

Previous chapters have considered the causes of a crisis and the five areas of leadership expertise that you can work to develop to be better prepared to manage after a crisis. The glue that will help to bring all of these elements together is your ability to build the right level of trust with stakeholders.

Last words

Leading after a crisis is one of the most challenging experiences a manager can expect to face but it can also be one of the most rewarding. I wish you all the best of success with your leadership journey. Just remember, always, to be careful with your assumptions.

References

Charan, R (2001) *What the CEO Wants You to Know: The little book of big business*, Crown Publications

Charan, R (2008) *What the Customer Wants You to Know: How everybody needs to think differently about sales*, Michael Joseph

Goffee, R and Jones, G (2006) *Why Should Anyone Be Led By You?* Harvard Business School Press

Greyser, S (1982) *Johnson & Johnson: The Tylenol tragedy*, Harvard Business Publishing

IDEO (2003) *IDEO Method Cards: 51 Ways to inspire design*, IDEO

Maister, D, Galford, R and Green, C (2000) *The Trusted Advisor*, Simon & Schuster Ltd

McCarty, J and Foecke, T (2008) *What Really Sank the Titanic: New forensic discoveries*, Citadel

Prahalad, C K (2004) *The Fortune at the Bottom of the Pyramid: Eradicating poverty through profits*, Wharton School Publishing

Pyhrr, P (1977) *Zero-base Budgeting: A practical management tool for evaluating expenses*, John Wiley & Sons Inc

Schoemaker, P and Gunther, R (2002) *Profiting from Uncertainty: Strategies for succeeding no matter what the future brings*, Free Press

Sull, D and Escobari, M (2005) *Brahma Versus Antartica: Reversal of fortune in Brazil's beer market*, London Business School case study

Useem, M (1999) *The Leadership Moment*, Random House USA Inc

Index

NB: page numbers in *italic* indicate figures or tables

360° view of business 59, 60, 61, 68, 167

Ackoff, R 45
Apple 44–45
  iPod/iPhone 45
assumptions 25–31, 36–38, 191
  see also crises *and* stakeholders
  changes to 179
  about future cash generation 57–58
  lack of respect for 27, 29
  for managing risk 37–38
authenticity 2, 16–18, *17*, 186
  see also communication

balance 7–8
  wobble board analogy for 8, 26, 82–83, *83*, 100, 104, 167–68, *168*
banking 27–30, 30, 116–17, 130
  and company borrowing 54–57

budget process 101–04
  see also zero-based budgeting
business licences
  formal/informal 48–51, *49*
  social 50, 51
business results, delivering 3–4, *5*

case studies
  London Business School 2005 on cost control 41
  on Tylenol (1982) by Stephen Greyser (Harvard Business Review, 1982) 155
  see also Tylenol
cash flow (and) 11–12, 125–48, *134*
  actual 129–30
  vs forecast 129–30
  cash conversion 127
  forecasting 104–06, 128–30
    see also cash forecasting and management tools
  recovery plan 116

restoration of understanding
of 128
time management 11–12,
126–31 *see also main entry*
velocity 127
cash forecasting and management
tools 131–48
accounts payable 144–45
accounts receivable 143–44
capital spending 141
cash committees 131–33
cash improvement
opportunities 138–39
forecasting 133–35, *134*
inventory and work-in-
progress 145–47
time and cash before
accounting 135–38
trapped cash 139–40
working capital 141–43
cash management 106–12, *107, 108*
change, lack of management
sensitivity to 120
Charan, R 127
communication 184–87, *186*
authentic 2, 16–18, *17*, 186
see also trust, rebuilding
and intimacy-building
potential 187–89
and PowerPoint 186
with stories/Q&A 186
core business skills 2–3, 5, 10–13,
19, 125–60 *see also individual
subject entries and* time
management
cash flow 11–12, 125–48, *134*
cost base restructuring 11, 12–13,
157–60
crises, developing strategy
after 11, 12, 151–54
sales/sales income,
maintaining 11, 13, 154–57
corporate breakdown (and) 34, 53,
59–69

adverse outcome from critical legal
judgement 60, 65–67
failure of IT implementation
60–65
lack of 360° view of business 59,
60, 61, 68
unbalanced economics/
incentivization 59, 60
cost base (and) 112–15
buffet analogy 114
restructuring 11, 12–13, 157–60
see also cost reduction tactics
Zero Based Budgeting
(ZBB) 114–15
cost reduction tactics 158–60 *see
also* management systems/tools
activity-based costing (ABC) 159
business process
reengineering 159
economies of scale 159
offshoring 159
outsourcing 159
'salami slicing' 159
Six Sigma 159
total quality management
(TQM) 150, 159
crises, developing strategy after 11,
12, 151–54
with customer/market-driven
opportunity strategy 153–54
pragmatic capitalist approach
to 152–53
crises, external causes of 33–51,
179 *see also* assumptions *and*
stakeholders
customer priorities (and) 34,
39–43
cost control 40
perceptions of risk 41
spending patterns 39–41, 43
economic cycles 33, 35–9
innovation – product, technology
and business model (and) 34,
43–48
gemba 47

Index

paranoia 48
systems thinking 45–46
and operational vs financial leverage 42–43
outside intervention/changes 34, 48–51, *49*
and formal/informal licences 48–51, *49* *see also* business licences
risk areas in 49–50, *49*
crises, internal drivers of 34, 53–73, 179
broken promises 34, 53, 54–59 *see also* banking
corporate breakdown 34, 53, 59–69 *see also main entry*
and examples of lack of foresight 72–73
lack of sensitivity 34, 53, 71–73
management optimism 34, 53, 69–71
crises, leading after (and) 1–19 *see also individual subject entries and* promises
authentic communication 2, 16–18, *17* *see also* communication, authentic
core business skills 2, 10–13
leadership expertise, areas of 2–5
promises, making the right 2, 6–8
recovery plan 18–19
relationships and results 2, 13–16, *14*
trust, rebuilding 2, 16–18, *17*
crises 21–31
definition of 21–22, 29, 31, 33
developing strategy after 151–54
example of 27–31, *30*
external causes of *see* crises, external causes of
global environment and resources 68
internal drivers of *see* crises, internal drivers of

leadership key roles after 15
managing risk of 37–39 *see also* assumptions
preventing 31
starting after *see* recovery planning
triggers of 22–31, *24*, *25*, *30*, 34–35 *see also* stakeholders
customer aces 9, *9*, *92*, 93, 94–99, *97*
customers/consumers 6, 22, 84–86, 167, *168*
assumptions of 96–98
and lean thinking 120–21
and recovery plans 115–16
tipping points of 94–95
understanding 120–21
see also IDEO Method Cards
views/viewpoints of 93, *97*, 98–99

definition(s) of
crisis 21–22, 29, 48, 179
leadership as followership 162, *163*
trust 180–81
delivering results *see* results, delivering

employees 6–7, 22, 87, 166–67, *168*
understanding feelings of 117–19

figures
balancing skills: making promises *83*
cash management models *107*, *108*
delivering results after crisis *14*
discretionary effort, tool for *164*
leadership *162*
making promises *7*, *100*
management wobble board *168*
measuring business trust *181*
proforma R&P cash flow *124*
Trivial Pursuits™ model *92*
trust equation *17*, *181*
viewpoints *9*

forecast process   104–06
   and cash flow forecasting   105–06
Fortune at the Bottom of the Pyramid, The   70

Goffee, R   80
Google   72–73, 137

IDEO Method Cards   121
   and Five Whys? exercise   121
intelligence, gathering military/secret   90–91
inventory and work in progress   145–47

Joiner, J   14
Jones, G   80

key performance indicators (KPIs)   130–31
   financial   136

leaders, key roles for   22
leadership approach, extremes of   177–78
   Big Picture Person   177
   Red Adair (lead from the front)   177–78
   Silk Suit   178
leadership expertise, areas of   2–19, 80–81 *see also individual subject entries and* promises
   and balance/wobble board analogy   8 *see also* balance
   business results, delivering   3–4, 81
   core business skills   3, 5, 10–13, 81
   expanding insight and knowledge *see* viewpoints, multiple new
   promises, making the right   2–3, 6–8, 7, 19, 80
   rebuilding trust with authentic communication   2, 5, 81
Leadership Moment, The   76

lean thinking   120–21, 137–38, 150–51, 175–76
   and choices to be made   176

McCarty, J   35
Maister, D   181
management sensitivity   43
management systems/tools   175
   balanced scorecard   150
   lean thinking   120–21, 137–38, 150–51, 175–76
   open innovation   175
   Six Sigma   150, 159, 175
   standard operating procedures (SOPs)   174, 175
   total quality management (TQM)   150, 159
   Toyota Production System   150
Markides, C   187
models
   $100 cash management   106–11, *107, 108*
   Nestlé economic profit/key drivers model   111–12
   operating model for delivering results   14–15, *164*, 167–68, 174–76
   QVSI (quality, value, service, innovation)   84–86

optimism, unhealthy   69–71

planning, scenario   120
planning, strategic   120–21
Phyrr, P   114
Popularly Positioned Product strategy (Nestlé)   40
Prahalad, C K   70
Profiting from Uncertainty   120
promises   2–3, 6–9, *9*, 19, 24–25, *25*, 29–30, 75–76, 80, 81–88, *83, 92, 93*, 99–106, *100*, 179
   broken   53, 54–59
   and budget process   101–04
   delivering on   22

and forecast process 104–06
making and delivery of 101
re-balancing 48

QVSI (quality, value, service, innovation) model 84–86

recovery planning 18–19, 75–88, 116–23, 179, 185–91
see also employees; promises; stakeholders *and* trust, rebuilding
appropriately 77
by building trust 78–79
by buying time 76–77
first steps in 79–81
and IDEO Method Cards 121
just do it method for 167
key point in 77–78
and lean thinking 120–21
by making new promises 88
by making right promises 81–88, *83*
and productivity/incentives 118–19
stakeholder analysis for 181–82, *181*
resources, best use of 90
results, delivering 5, 13–16, 19, 161–78, *163, 164 see also* lean thinking
through actions 171–74
through better relationships 167–68, *168*
by discretionary effort 163–64, *164*, 167
operating model for 14–15, *164*, 167–68, 174–76
overview of 165–69, 168
and planning/monitoring results 170–71
through possibilities and relationships 176–78
by setting targets 14, *14*, 169–7171

and standard operating procedures (SOPs) 174
and strategy 164–65

sales/sales income, maintaining 11, 13, 154–57
through confidence of sales staff 155–56
through external communication 156–57
with marketing and product development teams 156
scenario planning 120–22
Schoemaker, P 120
Scott, L 83
stakeholder analysis 181–82, *181*
see also trust
stakeholders 6–7, 22–23, 75–78, 115–19, 167–68, *181*, 182–84
assumptions of 23–26, *24*, 28–29, 31, 35, 36–37, 78, 96–97
change in 48, 179
communicating value to 184–86
customers/consumers 6, 22, 84–86 *see also main entry*
employees 6–7, 22, 87, 117–18
identifying key 23
interactions with 187–89
investors and lenders 6, 22, 54, 86–87, 130, 167, *168*
promises, not intentions to 58–59
and recovery plans 116
and perceived risk 189–91
promises to 24–25, *25*, 29–30, 48, 75–76
broken 53, 54–59
and QVSI – quality, value, service, innovation 84–86
suppliers 7, 22, 88, 167, *168*
standard operating procedures (SOPs) 174
Sull, D 41
supply chain tools 120
systems thinking 45–46

tables
  2005 banking example *30*
  promises to stakeholders *25*
  risk areas in relation to customers and consumers *49*
  stakeholder assumptions *24*
  taking customer's viewpoint *97*
Telles, M 41
time management 11–12, 125–48, *134*
tipping points 94–95
Titanic disaster 27, 36–37, 61
  factors contributing to 35
trust, rebuilding 16–18, *17*, 19, 179–91 *see also* authenticity; communication *and* trust
  benefits less costs = value 184–7, *186*
  through intimacy 187–89
  and perceived risk 189–91
  and post-crisis trust levels 180
trust 181–83
  and communication 191
  equation 17–18, *17, 181*, 184
  stakeholder analysis for 181–82, *181*
Trusted Advisor, The 181
Tuval, Y 181
Tylenol 155, 156–57

UBS Wealth Management 'You & Us' campaign 187–88
Useem, M 76

viewpoints, multiple new 2, 3, 5, 8–10, 19, 80, 89–123, *92*
  customer aces *see main entry and* customers/consumers
  flesh and blood *9, 92*, 93, 115–19 *see also* employees *and* stakeholders
  follow the money *9, 92*, 93, 106–12, *107, 108 see also* cash flow *and* cash management
  imagine new futures *9, 92*, 93, 119–23 *see also* recovery planning
  lean not mean *9, 92*, 93, 112–15 *see also* cost base
  making promises you can keep *9, 9, 92*, 93, 99–106, *100 see also* promises
  Trivial Pursuit™ approach to 91–93, *92*

What Really Sank the Titanic 35
What the CEO Wants You to Know 127
What the Customer Wants You to Know 127
Why Should Anybody be Led by You? 80

zero based budgeting (ZBB) 104, 114–15, 141, 160